A BIOGRAPHICAL STUDY OF

WALTER SCOTT

AMERICAN FRONTIER
EVANGELIST

A BIOGRAPHICAL STUDY OF

WALTER SCOTT

AMERICAN FRONTIER
EVANGELIST

by

WILLIAM A. GERRARD III

Cover Art by Paula Nash Giltner

Library of Congress Catalog Number: 91-77278
International Standard Book Number: 0-89900-405-9

TABLE OF CONTENTS

91538

FOREWORD

This work on Walter Scott is a revision of an earlier doctoral dissertation in the Department of Theological Studies, Emory University, Atlanta, Georgia. It is the intent of the revised work to see Walter Scott's life and thought in light of his own times and the currents of thought prevalent in the early and middle nineteenth century. The writer hopes that it will be of interest to those who are concerned with the origins of the Disciples movement and the relevance Walter Scott may have to the church in the latter decades of the twentieth century.

ACKNOWLEDGMENTS

In the course of writing this work, many persons were helpful, and to these persons I wish to express my grateful appreciation .

Dr. Dwight E. Stevenson and Dr. Richard M. Pope at the Lexington Theological Seminary gave valuable insights into Disciples History and the thought of Walter Scott. Mr. Roscoe M. Pierson, Librarian at the Lexington Theological Seminary, was very helpful in making available primary source materials.

Appreciation is expressed to many persons at the Disciples of Christ Historical Society for making resource materials available and assisting in the research. My thanks are offered to Rev. Roland K. Huff, David and Donna McWhirter, and Dr. James M. Seale.

I acknowledge with gratitude Dr. Channing R. Jeschke and Ms. Sahah Myers, Librarians at the Pitts Theology Library, Emory University. They made available the valuable resource material without which this work could not have been completed.

In the course of writing my doctoral dissertation on Walter Scott, I am most appreciative of my professors at Emory University who guided me and gave valuable theological insights. My thanks are thus extended to Dr. James M. May, Dr. Jack S. Boozer, Dr. Fred B. Craddock, Dr. Don E. Saliers, and Dr. Theodore H. Runyon, Jr.

I wish also to thank Dr. Richard L. Harrison, Jr., Dean of the Disciples Divinity House, Vanderbilt University, for reading the entire manuscript and making valuable suggestions.

Finally, a word of thanks goes to Ms. Jeann Greenway who typed the manuscript and made many suggestions on style.

INTRODUCTION

The present century, then, is characterized by these three successive steps, which the lovers of our Lord Jesus have been enabled to make, in their return to the original institution. First the Bible was adopted as sole authority in our assemblies, to the exclusion of all other books. Next the Apostolic order was proposed. Finally the True Gospel was restored.

Walter Scott, *The Gospel Restored*, Preface, pp. v-vi.

Penning these words, Walter Scott gave a panoramic view of the Disciples of Christ movement or "New Reformation" as it emerged in the early decades of the nineteenth century. Thomas Campbell had taken the first step in claiming the Bible as primary for the faith of the church and Christian union. His life-long friend and co-worker, Alexander Campbell, was responsible for the second step, the restoration of the "Ancient Order" of the church. Finally, he himself took credit for restoring to the church the "True" or "Ancient Gospel" as it was preached in the early church. These three personalities, along with Barton W. Stone, were responsible for bringing into being a new religious movement that has been rich and varicolored because of the distinctive contributions of each of these pioneer fathers. From humble beginnings the movement has grown into one of the largest that is indigenous to American soil.

A number of biographical and theological studies have been done on Thomas and Alexander Campbell and Barton W. Stone. This is not true in the case of Walter Scott. The earliest work on Scott was by William Baxter in 1874. The most current biography of Scott was written by Dwight E. Stevenson over forty years ago and published in 1946. Since that time several unpublished theses have dealt with various aspects of Scott's life and thought. These have added invaluably to our knowledge of the man, his thought, and the role he played as the Disciples of Christ came into being. In all of these works, however, no serious attempt has been made to relate Scott to his philosophical and theological heritage or to show how this heritage influenced the major directions in his theology.

It is hoped that the present writing will add to our overall knowledge of Scott in this regard. We will seek to get on the inside of his mind and see the world, the Bible, and the Christian faith through his eyes. This enthusiastic and tireless evangelist was a man who, like other creative minds, was a child of his time and expressed himself in terms of the thought patterns of his own day. In order to understand him we need to answer some basic questions. Who was this man? What were his passions, those issues that touched him deeply, those religious ideas and forces he opposed? What was going on in nineteenth century America at the time he lived and preached? What were those philosophical, theological, and cultural forces that impinged upon him and gave shape to the ideas about which he wrote and preached?

Viewed from the vantage point of the latter decades of the twentieth century, Walter Scott may appear to be light years away from us in terms of how he expressed his convictions. Some may look upon him as an anachronism. What can he possibly say that has meaning or relevance to us today? Yet, as we look more closely at this pioneer evangelist we may well see that in significant ways he was miles ahead of his time in terms of how he thought, what his grand vision was, what he was able to accomplish.

It is the intent of this study to portray the true man, his genius, and how he has contributed to those children in the various streams flowing from the nineteenth century Reformation. We may see Scott's thought centered around certain bedrock truths that are essential for the Christian faith in any age. It may be that his insights and formative principles are timely and have relevance for the era in which we are living. If this is true, then Walter Scott not only deserves to be heard anew but also to be called one of the "Four Founding Fathers" of the Christian Church or Disciples of Christ. His legacy may rightfully be claimed by his heirs in the Christian

Church (Disciples of Christ), the Independent Christian Churches, and the Church of Christ.

William A. Gerrard III.

Atlanta, Georgia
November, 1991

CHAPTER ONE

A SCOTSMAN'S PILGRIMAGE IN AMERICA

I immediately cut all other connections, abandoned my projected Editorship, dissolved my academy; left my church, left my family, dropt the bitterest tear over my infant household that ever escaped from my eyes, and set out under the simple conduct of Jesus Christ to make an experiment of what is now styled the Ancient Gospel.

Walter Scott, *The Evangelist* 1 (1832): 94.

As the curtain came up on the nineteenth century, America was like a giant awakening from a sleep and stretching his muscles. It was being transformed from a group of loosely knit colonies into a sprawling young nation. America was a nation on the move — growing, changing, being molded. Railroads and canals, textile mills and cotton gins, all came to symbolize the social and economic transformation that was taking place.

After the War of 1812, waves of immigration brought new settlers into the Ohio Valley. The roads westward swarmed with wagons and horses, cattle and sheep. On the Allegheny, Monongahela, and Ohio Rivers paddle boats and crude rafts brought scores of families into the new area. Ohio, Kentucky, Tennessee, and Illinois were called "the West," the raw American frontier. Towns sprang up almost overnight; new churches formed. From the eastern states there was a great population movement into the northeastern section of Ohio, called the Western Reserve.

They pressed restlessly into the West, seeking new homes, new lives, new ventures on the ever-receding frontier. A new nation gave birth to a new consciousness. A new age dedicated to liberty and freedom of the common man and woman had been born. The ordinary person of the day possessed a basic sense of worth. This person had possibilities, a sense of optimism and hope for a bright future. It was generally believed that one's reason could solve the basic human problems. This child of a new age was important not only as a soul to be saved for eternity but equally a being deserving happiness and a good life on his or her earthly pilgrimage.

Into this turbulent and ever-changing scene moved the great surging waves of evangelical revivalism. New religious sects, cults and movements dotted the landscape. Viewing the religious scene in early nineteenth century America was like looking through a kaleidoscope and seeing different patterns emerge and change shape. It was a true heyday of sectarianism. There were the perfectionists and adventists, the Swedenborgians and spiritualists. Communal societies were a major cultural force in the religious pluralism of the day. Shakers and Rappites, the Oneida and Hopedale Communities all flourished for a period of time.

This was America in 1827, the year Walter Scott "cut all other connections" as he described it. He was on the eve of embarking on a new venture as Evangelist for the Mahoning Baptist Association. In so doing, he entered the arena of American revivalism.

If America was to have her soul converted, so it was reasoned by many, it must be done by the revivalists. Wave after wave of religious excitement and revivalism made the state of New York notorious as the "burned-over district," where orthodoxy would not prosper, though twisted forms of religion would. As the revivals coursed through the early years of the nineteenth century, camp meetings were the tool used especially by the Methodists and Baptists.

Prominent among the revivalists who were trying to sway the masses were Peter Cartwright, Lyman Beecher, and Asahel Nettleton. None were more spectacular than Charles Grandison Finney, the peripatetic evangelist. In 1827 Finney brought his revival to Philadelphia and there reaped a grand harvest. Congregation after congregation were held spellbound by his searching, hypnotic eyes and stentorian voice, all of which he used with the skill of a trained actor. Under the magical spell of his preaching, their souls melted, and they came to the "anxious bench" confessing their sins and seeking heaven's mercy.

The year 1827 was a turning point in the life of Joseph Smith, an unschooled farmer in Palmyra, New York. He claimed that the angel Moroni had appeared to him in a vision and led him to a cache of golden plates inscribed in reformed Egyptian hieroglyphics. To aid him in his task of reading them, he was shown a set of seer stones, Urim and Thummim. Late in 1827, Joseph Smith began to translate the mysterious tablets with his wife as copyist. Then in March 1830, the *Book of Mormon* was put on sale, and a new religion was born.

For the nation, her new religions and the revivalists, and for Walter Scott especially, 1827 was a high point. It was a year for new beginnings and adventure, as he set out on his evangelistic crusade among the Baptist churches on the Western Reserve. Little did he know what lay in store for him during the years 1827-1830, or what he would be able to accomplish. As time would tell, this three year period thrust him into a prominent role among the Disciples and gave him a claim to fame in the annals of the Reformation of the nineteenth century.

This, then, is the story of the man — his life, his thought, his achievements — Walter Scott, American Frontier Evangelist.

Early Life and Education in Scotland (1796-1818)

Walter Scott[1] was born on October 31, 1796, in the town of Moffatt, county of Dumfriesshire, Scotland. In the Scott family there were ten children, five sons and five daughters, Walter being the sixth child.[2] His parents, John and Mary Innes Scott, were Presbyterians, members of the Church of Scotland, and raised their children in this faith. Early in life Walter displayed talent and brilliance, to the delight of his parents. In order to encourage the development and education of their gifted son, the Scotts saved from their meagre resources and were able to send him to the University of Edinburgh. John and Mary Innes wished their son to become a Presbyterian minister in the Church of Scotland, and toward this end he directed his efforts and studies at the university.[3] Through a strange turn of circumstances, however, Walter Scott was never ordained a Presbyterian minister in Scotland. The course of his life was to follow a different path.

Sometime during the years 1812-1818, Walter Scott attended the University of Edinburgh. It is uncertain whether or not he actually graduated from the University. The University records for that time are very scanty. Furthermore, a number of different young men by the name of Walter Scott attended between 1808-1818.[4] It is fairly certain that he finished his studies there in 1818.[5] Since he was preparing for the ministry, he pursued a course in the Arts. The first year course consisted of Humanity (Latin), Greek, Logic and Metaphysics, Mathematics, and Moral Philosophy.[6] It is also highly probable that he enrolled for other subjects that were taught at Edinburgh at that time: Hebrew, Divinity and Ecclesiastical History, Natural Philosophy, Universal Civil History and Antiquities, Rhetoric, and Belles Lettres.[7]

At Edinburgh Walter Scott received an excellent education in the Arts and was introduced to the larger world of learning, scholarship, and culture. There he acquired the fundamental linguistic tools that would serve him well in his preaching, teaching, writing, and editorial work; these included Greek, Latin, and Hebrew. These initial formative years at the University of Edinburgh sharpened his mind, made him thirsty for knowledge, and enhanced his capacity to think in a larger historical, philosophical, and theological framework.

Early Years in America (1818-1827)

An invitation came to the Scott family from George Innes, his mother's brother, to send one of the boys to America. He gave them assurance that he would assist their son in advancing his career here. From among the members of the family, Walter was chosen.[8] Leaving Greenock, Scotland, he arrived in New York on July 7, 1818. Through the assistance of George Innes, Scott secured employment at the Union Academy of Jamaica, Long Island, where he taught English, Greek, and Latin.[9]

Scott was in New York for less than a year before restlessness took its toll and he journeyed to Pittsburgh, arriving there on May 7, 1819.[10] To his surprise and delight he met George Forrester,[11] a fellow Scotsman, who had a small congregation and also conducted an academy. This congregation, which had come into being primarily under the influence of the writings of James A. Haldane and Robert Haldane, had as its purpose a restoration of the beliefs and practices of the primitive New Testament church. Scott was soon to discover that this church differed markedly from his rearing in the Church of Scotland. Not only did Scott begin to teach in the academy as an assistant to Forrester, but he also associated himself with this Haldanean congregation. A warm friendship developed between the two, resulting in his decision to join the church and be baptized by Forrester in 1819.[12] This year with George Forrester was significant for the promising young teacher and preacher. Under Forrester's influence and personal guidance, Scott began to develop a different view of baptism and the Bible. In his quest for an overall, comprehensive understanding of the Christian faith, Forrester was instrumental in introducing him to a different theological perspective and giving a new direction to his thinking. The following year, 1820, Forrester drowned while swimming in the Allegheny River, leaving the church and the academy to the care of his gifted associate.[13]

Following this tragedy to his personal friend, Scott stayed in Pittsburgh for several years serving in a dual role — pastor to the Haldanean congregation and head of the academy. These were years of intensive Bible study and personal questing, as the yeast of learning and the Spirit were fermenting new ideas in his fertile mind. Access to Forrester's library aided him in his biblical studies and also exposed him to a wider range of theological works. In later years, he recalled the importance of this period of study and specifically some of the books from Forrester's library that had made an impact on his thinking.

> He left behind him also an excellent library containing many volumes on Holy Scripture, as Benson on the Epistles, McKnight's Harmony of the Gospels, Catchbull's Notes, Haldane's Works, Campbell on the Four

Gospels, Locke's Reasonableness of Christianity, McKnight on the Epistles, Carson's Works with those of Wardlaw, Glass, Sandeman, Letters published by Eld. Errett, New York, and many other valuable treatises, which, with Bishop Newcome's Harmony of the Gospels, Towers, Warburton and Newton, made the author acquainted with the advance steps of the modern reformers — Carson, Warlaw, Haldane, Glass, and Sandeman, all of whose efforts were merely ecclesiastical.[14]

In 1821, there came to his attention a pamphlet, *On Baptism*,[15] written by Henry Errett, a member of a New York City congregation of "Scotch Baptists." This aroused his curiosity! Who were these "Scotch Baptists"? As he would soon discover they were the branch of the Sandemanians who practiced baptism by immersion.[16] Thinking that a visit to this congregation would be beneficial, he journeyed to New York and spent several months with them.[17] There he had an opportunity to attend a series of lectures on the four Gospels given by Errett.[18]

Following his trip to New York, Scott returned to Pittsburgh and became tutor of a private school in the home of Robert Richardson.[19] A short time after this, while engaged in his study and teaching, he came to the conception that was to be the cornerstone of his theology and the centerpiece of his biblical and theological writings. Scott concluded that the central point of the whole Christian faith and the core of the Bible is the truth that Jesus Christ is the Son of God, the Messiah. Viewing his newly discovered truth as a precious jewel to be treasured, he called it the "Golden Oracle."[20]

During the winter of 1821-1822, while residing in the

Richardson home, Walter Scott met Alexander Campbell, who at that time lived in Bethany, Virginia, and was a member of the Redstone Baptist Association. A congeniality and warm friendship developed between Campbell and Scott that would continue for the next forty years. Although they did not always agree, the two men labored together in the new movement of which they were leaders in its initial years. This close relationship found expression in the editorial field. Discussing a projected periodical, Campbell confided in his friend, "Walter, I want to begin publishing a new paper, and I'm going to call it 'The Christian.' What do you think?"

"Why," Scott mused, "that is fine, but let me make a suggestion if I may. Since you are laboring among the Baptists, wouldn't it be prudent to call it 'The Christian Baptist'? More of the Baptists would read it, wouldn't they?"

"Splendid idea, Walter," Campbell responded, "it shall be called 'The Christian Baptist.' "[21] In 1823, Campbell began publishing *The Christian Baptist*,[22] a monthly periodical. During the next seven years at Campbell's invitation, Scott contributed a number of articles to *The Christian Baptist* and signed all of them simply as "Philip." Scott believed that they were about to launch a new religious movement in the church, similar in many ways to the Reformation of the sixteenth century that shook the church at its foundations. He viewed his friend Alexander Campbell as the Luther or prophetic voice of their movement and himself as the Melanchthon.

On January 3, 1823, Walter Scott and Sarah Whitsette

were married, and in the next ten years six children blessed the marriage.[23] In the summer of 1826 Scott and the family moved to Steubenville, Ohio, and lived there for one year; following this they went to Canfield, Ohio, in the fall of 1827, residing there for four years. These years in Ohio were epoch-making for the life of Scott. Besides teaching school and ministering to his congregation, the most significant chapter of his life was as Evangelist for the Mahoning Baptist Association from 1827-1830.

With the Mahoning Baptist Association (1827-1830)

Scott first attended a meeting of the Mahoning Baptist Association[24] held at Canfield, Ohio, in August 1826. This was at the invitation of Alexander Campbell, who had been affiliated with it since 1824.[25] The Association was first organized in 1820 by Adamson Bentley and consisted of ten Baptist churches that had their locus in the northeastern section of Ohio known as the "Connecticut Western Reserve."[26] Then in 1826, six other churches joined the Association.[27] This loose federation of churches, which had been heavily influenced by Campbell's reforming views, met together annually.

The Western Reserve was to be Scott's field of evangelism for the next three years. It was frontier country, the cutting edge of the West, and an area teeming with excitement. Walter Scott not only shared in the excitement on the Reserve but also created some of it himself.

In the late eighteenth and early nineteenth centuries, there was a large population movement westward.

From Connecticut, Massachusetts, New York, Pennsylvania, and Virginia there was a steady stream of settlers moving into the Ohio Valley and the Western Reserve. Population increase meant the emergence of small towns and with them new churches. Still, there were more and more souls to be saved! Who would preach to them? Who would win them for Christ? The more thoughtful of the revivalists and other churchmen could almost hear the Lord Jesus Himself speaking directly to them beseechingly: "I tell you, lift up your eyes, and see how the fields are already white for harvest" (John 4:35). William Warren Sweet, in his study of this era of American religious history, has assessed the challenging situation facing the churches:

> These were critical years in the history of the American churches, for the future of the nation as well as the future of religion in America was largely to be determined by the way in which organized religion met the problem of the new West. And the churches which met this problem most adequately were the ones destined to become the great American churches.[28]

The single most prominent feature of frontier American religion, and especially of the Western Reserve, was revivalism. In the early years of the nineteenth century, the camp meetings associated with the Great Western Revival spread northward throughout Kentucky and into the Western Reserve with great fervor. In terms of denominations, the Baptists and Methodists were the predominant ones on the Reserve.[29] Most of the churches affiliated with the Mahoning Baptist Association were formed during this evangelistic ferment between 1800 and 1820.[30]

Population surges, new towns, new churches, the revivalists — all mixed together to paint the landscape. But all did not mix well; peace did not reign in the churches or between them! The attitudes of individualism, non-conformity, and self-reliance in the frontier mind were contributing factors in the emergence of the sects and denominational schisms. Although the Baptists and Methodists were the largest numerically, many other denominations and small sects existed on the Western Reserve. Because of divergent interpretations of the Scriptures, irreconcilable differences often developed between various factions in the churches, resulting in permanent parties, schisms, or the emergence of sects. Hairsplitting theological subtleties and rigid creedal formulations took their toll in fragmenting the churches. Strife, envy, and contention characterized to a large extent the religious climate of the day. These groups sought to fortify their denominational and sectarian walls by maintaining the correctness of their respective doctrinal formulations or ecclesiastical structures. In this milieu of pluralism and sectarian rivalry, little or no thought was given to the idea or possibility of Christian union.

A pronounced feature of the Mahoning Baptist Association was the significance attached to creeds. The Association as a whole adopted a creed, and the individual churches in the Association each had a creed. In order to be voted membership in the Association, each church was required to submit a suitable creed. All of these creeds, which were thoroughly Calvinistic, were modeled after the Philadelphia Confession of Faith, formulated at the Baptist Association on September 25, 1742.[31]

The particular doctrines expressed in the creed of the Mahoning Baptist Association were spoken of in the religious parlance of the day as TULIP Calvinism, an acronym standing for total depravity of human nature, unconditional predestination, limited atonement, irresistible grace, and the perseverance of the saints. In accordance with this Calvinistic orientation, stress was placed on the supernatural operation of the Holy Spirit in one's conversion and the feelings associated with it. One gained membership in the church by standing before the gathered congregation and relating in detail an acceptable conversion experience.

Affirmed in the creed also were baptism by immersion and belief in the Scriptures as the only rule of faith and practice.[32] Even though the creed asserted the importance of the Scriptures, the principal emphasis was placed on the Holy Spirit's special operation in conversion. Unless one had this conversion experience, so the reasoning went, the Bible was powerless to convince or persuade the mind. It was not uncommon to hear one of the good brothers or sisters say: "The Word of God is a dead letter, a sealed book. I would just as soon depend on an old almanac for conversion as the Bible, unless the Holy Spirit directly acts on your soul and opens your mind."[33] It was to persons with this mind set that Scott preached when he first began his work among the churches in the Association. No wonder their ears picked up when they heard this Scotsman preach! His message was different than what they had heard before. He beseeched them to look to the words of Scripture themselves — read, listen, think, decide for themselves.

In order to have a clearer picture of Scott's relationship with the Mahoning Baptist Association, one must consider the growing influence of Alexander Campbell. From the time of Campbell's affiliation with the Association in 1824, he became increasingly active in promoting his views for the restoration of Primitive Christianity and the sole authority of the Scriptures in matters of faith and church practice. Included in Campbell's program were his opposition to all non-Scriptural practices, unauthorized church associations, and creeds as tests of fellowship. Through the pages of *The Christian Baptist* and in his other writings, Campbell's views spread not only among the churches participating in the Mahoning Association but also throughout the Western Reserve and Ohio. During these years a party calling themselves "Reformers" and espousing the views of Campbell developed within the Association. Numbered among their ranks were William Hayden, A.S. Hayden, Adamson Bentley, Jacob Osborne, and John Henry. Soon groups of Reformers were to be found in almost every Baptist church in the West, and in many instances they began to separate from the Baptists to form their own congregations. By 1825, many of the churches in the Association had abandoned all of the articles of faith in their creeds except the one affirming the sole authority of the Scriptures for all matters of faith and church practice.[34] Alexander Campbell had plowed the ground well before Scott began to preach. Into the freshly plowed earth, Scott planted the seeds of the Word!

When Walter Scott first attended the Association's annual meeting in 1826, Campbell was the first preacher to speak. Although Scott was neither a Baptist nor a

member of the Association, through ministerial cour-
tesy he was extended the invitation to preach at the
Sunday morning service on August 27. Preaching from
Matthew 11, he spoke with great eloquence and power,
his Scottish accent holding them enthralled and making
a lasting impression on the assembly.[35] Little did they
realize on that day that they would hear this young
Scotsman herald the Word many times in the years to
come!

At this time most of the Association churches were in
dire need of strengthening. Although the principles of
Campbell's reform were present as a ferment in the
churches, the churches themselves were not gaining
appreciably in numerical strength. Some of the churches
were lukewarm, others cold or dying. Robert Richardson stated the problem confronting the churches.

> There had indeed been an almost entire neglect of evan-
> gelization on the part of the few churches which were
> originally connected with Mr. Campbell in his reforma-
> tory efforts. They had not a single itinerant preacher,
> and, although they made great progress in biblical
> knowledge, they gained comparatively few converts.[36]

One of the most significant events for the Mahoning
Baptist Association, and a landmark for Scott himself,
occurred at the annual meeting held at New Lisbon,
Ohio, on August 23-25, 1827. A proposal was presented
to the Association that in view of the serious situation
facing the churches, an evangelist should be employed
to travel among them. Whom would they select? After
due consideration the Association voted unanimously
that Walter Scott was the appropriate person. Furthermore, he should devote all of his time and energies to

the task.[37] Scott reasoned, "Should I accept or not?" It would mean giving up his church, his academy, leaving his family. He even had plans to start his own periodical, 'The Millennial Herald.' It was a challenge — preaching the age-old gospel for a new day.[38] Like young Isaiah in the temple, it was as though the Lord was saying to him, "Whom shall I send, and who will go for us?" Yes, this was it — God was calling him for the task, and there were souls to be saved. His answer echoed Isaiah's "Here I am! Send me" (Isa. 6:8).

Scott immediately began to travel and preach. His task was imposing, and he took it with all seriousness — preach the Word to save the lost and strengthen the churches in the Mahoning Association. As he started on his new venture the questions that loomed large in his mind were: "How does one preach the gospel as it was preached in the Early Church? What are the steps one must take in order to be saved?" On these questions Scott meditated and prayed. He searched the pages of Holy Scripture and talked with trusted friends. Finally, the luminous moment came! What had up until then been a dark cloud faded, and the light shone. Everything for which he had been searching fell into place and formed a harmonious whole. It was scriptural and reasonable. Basing his thinking on Acts 2:38, Scott saw that the preaching of the gospel followed an orderly sequence. One was to have faith, repent, and be baptized. Subsequent to this one received the remission of sins, the gift of the Holy Spirit, and the promise of eternal life. With this recovery of the scriptural plan of salvation, in Scott's thinking a new era in the church had dawned.[39]

Scott's first effort to preach his newly discovered plan

of salvation was at Steubenville, Ohio, although it was not within the bounds of the Association. On this occasion, he failed to gain the desired response from his hearers.[40] The Word fell on deaf ears! On November 18, 1827, however, Scott's preaching at New Lisbon, Ohio, met with signal success. This sermon was singularly Scott's most important one in terms of content. Here, his evangelistic mission was launched on a course that would continue with enormous momentum throughout the time he was affiliated with the Association. What did he preach?[41]

The text for his sermon was Peter's confession at Caesarea Philippi as recorded in Matthew 16:16: "Thou art the Christ, the son of the living God." This was the central theme of the four Gospels. They were written to establish this fact as the central truth around which all other truths revolved. Type and prophecy from the Old Testament pointed to this declaration. Peter proclaimed this truth, and Christ gave him the keys to the kingdom of heaven; the keys of which Christ spoke were the conditions upon which persons might be pardoned and granted admission to the kingdom. When the multitudes assembled at Pentecost realized that Jesus was the Christ they cried out, "Men and brethren, what shall we do?" The answer was, "Repent, and be baptized, every one of you, in the name of Jesus Christ, for the remission of sins, and you shall receive the gift of the Holy Spirit." Making his application, Scott insisted that the conditions for salvation today are as they were at Pentecost. To receive the Word and obey it is to do what the souls at Pentecost did in response to Peter's invitation. In essence, the invitation was to accept Jesus Christ as the Son of God in faith, repent, and be baptized; remission of one's sins and the gift of the Holy Spirit would follow. The invitation being extended, a man by the name of William Amend accepted the offer and was baptized by Scott on the same day.[42]

Scott believed that this sermon and the response by William Amend were a momentous occasion, a landmark, in the history of the Christian Church. It was Scott's belief that the gospel, which had been distorted and lost to the church for all of these centuries, had now been restored. On this very day — November 18, 1827 — the original New Testament plan of salvation was preached and recovered for the church of his day. What Scott meant by the "Gospel Restored" was not simply preaching the good news and the steps in the plan of salvation, but making a practical application of it by baptizing someone for the remission of sins and receiving the gift of the Holy Spirit.

Scott's sermon at New Lisbon and his subsequent preaching had a sense of aliveness and freshness. The newness of his evangelistic appeal possessed an intensity and force as he preached in the churches of the Association. The exciting sense that he had rediscovered a long-lost truth that had lain dormant and covered with dust for centuries gave a quality of urgency to his efforts. He was convinced that his newly formulated plan of salvation would revitalize and strengthen the churches numerically. Indeed, it would unite all of the churches and save the world before Christ Himself came again! Scott's emphasis on the use of reason in one's approach to the Bible had a striking appeal to the common sense, practical mind of the frontiersmen in these churches that had been steeped in the Calvinistic theology and mode of conversion.

During his first year as Evangelist for the Association, Scott's efforts were marked by phenomenal success.[43] In all of the churches new converts were made. Under the impact of his preaching and evangelistic activity, many new churches were begun. Among Scott's converts for the year were ministers from other denominations. Often as they were won to Scott's ideas and new ways of presenting the gospel, they brought their entire congregations with them into the churches of the Association. The revival fires of the early nineteenth century, which had brought these churches into existence, were rekindled under the impact and forcefulness of Scott's fervent evangelistic preaching.

Even though Scott had been commissioned to preach for the Mahoning Baptist Association, his theological views and method of evangelism were at variance with the Calvinistic orientation of most Baptist churches. Scott's views were in essential agreement with those of Alexander Campbell and the Reformers who espoused his ideas. In a very real sense, then, Scott was championing the cause of this reforming element that had already gained a foothold in the churches. Through Scott's efforts, the cause of the Reformers in the Mahoning churches was strengthened and enhanced. Their influence became stronger and more pervasive as their beliefs became widely disseminated in the Baptist churches. In many instances, the churches established through Scott's efforts consisted solely of Reformers and those who embraced their sentiments.

In March of 1828, Alexander Campbell became concerned about reports of the young Scotsman's growing popularity and success on the Western Reserve. Since the Reserve was the stronghold of Campbell's reforming efforts and influence, he wanted to know the particulars of Scott's preaching among the churches. Alexander confided in his father, Thomas Campbell: "What do you think of our friend, Walter Scott, and his preaching in the Mahoning churches? After all, this is the heartland of our reform. If his preaching is not sound and biblical, all of our efforts could be dashed to pieces!"

Thomas responded, "Why don't I go and take a look. Maybe this fine young Scotsman is actually aiding our cause."

With an approving nod Alexander said, "Would you, father, and then let me know what you think. See if he is getting any lasting results."

Thomas Campbell journeyed to the Western Reserve and attended some of Scott's meetings. Hearing him preach and witnessing with great pleasure his evangelistic methods, Thomas Campbell was impressed. Being firmly convinced that what Scott was doing would give a positive thrust and advance the cause of the Reformers, he wrote to his son, Alexander:

> I perceive that theory and practice in religion, as well as in other things, are matters of distinct consideration. . . . We have long known the former (the theory), and have spoken and published many things "correctly concerning" the ancient gospel, its simplicity and perfect adaptation to the present state of mankind, for the benign and gracious purposes of his immediate relief and complete salvation; but I must confess that, in respect to the "direct exhibition" and "application" of it for that blessed purpose, I am at present for the first time upon the ground where the thing has appeared to

be "practically exhibited" to the proper purpose. . . .
Mr. Scott has made a bold push to accomplish this
object, by simply and boldly stating the ancient gospel,
and insisting upon it; . . . [44]

Alexander Campbell was satisfied; he had no misgivings. His friend Walter Scott was a true ally in forwarding the cause.

After Scott had engaged in a year of evangelistic activity on the Western Reserve, he attended the next annual meeting of the Association held in Warren, Ohio, on August 29, 1828.[45] Two of the highlights of this meeting were the report that Scott had been instrumental in baptizing over one thousand persons during the past year and his reappointment as Evangelist for the Association for another year.[46]

From 1828-1830, Scott's evangelistic efforts continued with unabated success. At the Association's annual meeting at Sharon, Pennsylvania, in August 1829, it was reported that another thousand converts had been added to the rolls of the churches. In August 1830, when the Association again met at Austintown, Ohio, one thousand more converts were reported as a result of Scott's successful evangelistic activities.[47]

During this three year period not only had over three thousand converts been made, but also radical changes had come about in the Association churches. Because of the increasing influence of the Reformers, the Association had ceased to be a Baptist organization except in name. All was not well, however. Reaction against the Reformers had set in among the orthodox in several of the Baptist associations. Opposition led to open hostility! The Beaver Association in Ohio went so far as to issue an anathema of the Mahoning Association in 1829, condemning them for heresy in scriptural interpretation. The Reformers countered decisively, determining to sever connections with the Baptists. The sentiment being expressed by the reforming element was that the churches should follow explicitly the pattern of government in the New Testament. No precedent could be found in Primitive Christianity for church associations such as the Baptists had formed, much less the issuing of official pronouncements like the Beaver anathema. The Reformers, therefore, reasoned that the Mahoning Baptist Association was without the sanction of Scripture and should be disbanded. If such were the case, an anathema against them would be virtually innocuous. Among the Reformers opposed to the continuation of the Association was Walter Scott, who had now become one of its most influential voices. Thus, the Association voted itself out of existence.

> John Henry, who had been among the first to enter the ranks of reform, and was already quite influential, moved "that the Mahoning Association, as an advisory council, or an ecclesiastical tribunal, should cease to exist." This was in accordance with the general feeling, but Mr. Campbell thinking the course proposed too precipitate, was on the point of rising to oppose the motion, when Walter Scott, seeing the strong current in favor of it, went up to him, and, placing a hand on each of his shoulders, begged him not to oppose the motion. He yielded; the motion passed unanimously; and it was then determined that, in the place of the Association, there should be an annual meeting for praise and worship, and to hear reports from laborers in the field of the progress of the good work.[48]

This action represented the formal separation of the

Reformers from their Baptist moorings. While within the confines of the Association, the Reformers were called "Campbellites" or "Scottites," whereas following the Association's decision to disband itself, they were most often called "Disciples."[49] Had this action not taken place, the movement spearheaded by Campbell and Scott might have continued only as a reforming influence within the Mahoning Baptist Association, perhaps diminishing in significance with the succeeding years. The dissolving of the Association represented one step, but a decisive one, in the emergence of what was to become a new force in American religion. From this time on, the churches that were advocating the reforming views constituted an autonomous, identifiable group. With this independent status and corporateness, they continued to make rapid progress. In 1832 the Reformers merged with the "Christians," a group in Kentucky with similar views and headed by Barton W. Stone.[50] Out of this union a new religious movement was born, variously called the Disciples Movement, the Stone-Campbell movement, or the Restoration movement. Like a child in the new age, it had a destiny awaiting and a hope to be fulfilled — union of the churches through a restoration of New Testament Christianity. Among the parents of this child none took more pride or labored more diligently for her than Walter Scott!

Middle and Latter Years (1830-1861)

Following this epoch-making three years as Evange-

37

list for the Mahoning Baptist Association, Scott engaged
in a number of different kinds of activities on behalf of
the New Reformation. Besides serving as minister of
several churches and conducting preaching tours, he
also wrote and edited periodicals. During the years
1831-1832, he and his family resided in Pittsburgh,
Cincinnati, and Carthage, Ohio. In 1831 Scott published
his first book, *A Discourse on the Holy Spirit*,[51] which was
so well-received that second and third editions followed. Scott also entered the arena of religious editing.
On January 2, 1832, he began issuing *The Evangelist*, a
monthly periodical, from his office in Cincinnati. For the
next twelve years, he continued to edit his periodical
from Cincinnati and Carthage.[52] During the summer of
1832, he was instrumental in organizing a church in
Carthage. Moving there in October 1833, he served as its
minister for the next twelve years. While residing there,
Scott wrote and published in 1836 one of his major theological works, *The Gospel Restored*.[53] This book was
offered in lieu of *The Evangelist* for that year.

In addition to his activities of writing and serving as
minister in several congregations, in 1836 Scott became
president of Bacon College in Georgetown, Kentucky,
one of the movement's institutions of higher education.
Bacon College was organized on November 10, 1836,
with the first classes meeting on November 14; the Kentucky legislature granted its first charter on February 23,
1837. The name Bacon College was selected in honor of
Sir Francis Bacon, who had elaborated the inductive scientific method.[54] Scott's inaugural address, *United States
System*,[55] was delivered in February 1837 after the college had been chartered.[56] He was only associated with

Bacon College for approximately one year, having consented to serve as its president on a "pro tempore" basis. He was interested in seeing the college launched and put on a sound financial basis, and his efforts were directed toward this end. During his tenure as president of the college, Scott taught courses and delivered a series of lectures.[57] After he had served for this short period of time, D.S. Burnett succeeded him as president in December 1837.[58]

Scott had suspended publishing his periodical, *The Evangelist*, in 1835 in order to write *The Gospel Restored*, serve as president of Bacon College, and co-edit *The Christian* with John T. Johnson from Georgetown, Kentucky. He resumed publishing *The Evangelist*[59] in January 1838, and continued to edit it from Carthage and Cincinnati until 1844. In April of that year he and his family moved back to Pittsburgh and lived there for five years. During this time he preached in two Pittsburgh churches and engaged in several revivals. Scott commenced editing a new weekly periodical, *The Protestant Unionist*,[60] in 1844 and continued its publication until 1847. Following the death of his wife on April 28, 1849, he returned to Cincinnati. There he merged *The Protestant Unionist* with J.T. Melish's *The Christian Age* to form *The Christian Age and Protestant Unionist*, which he and Melish edited jointly for a year.[61] This was the last venture in publishing periodicals for Scott, who had been engaged in the arena of religious editing for the past eighteen years.

For the remainder of his life Scott continued his writing, served as minister of a church, and conducted evangelistic tours. On November 29, 1849, an invitation was extended to him to become minister of the church at May's Lick, Kentucky, on a half-time basis.[62] He accepted the call and began his work there. On August 13,1850, he married a second time, to Nannie B. Allen, a member of the congregation. They remained at May's Lick for the next two years, during which time a daughter was born. In 1852, Scott and his family moved to Covington, Kentucky, where he opened a female academy.[63] During 1852 and the following year, he wrote and published two more books, *To Themelion: The Union of Christians*[64] and *He Nekrosis, or The Death of Christ*.[65] Both of these books went through several editions and were widely read among the Disciples and Christians. After his second wife died on November 18, 1854, Scott returned to May's Lick to live the remainder of his life. In 1855 he married a third time, to Eliza Sandridge, also a member of the May's Lick church.[66] While residing at May's Lick, he preached frequently at the church there,[67] conducted evangelistic tours, and wrote his final theological work, *The Messiahship*, which was published in 1859.

During these latter years, Scott's thoughts turned more and more to the nation and the storm clouds he saw on the immediate horizon. He readily perceived in the events of the day the approach of the Civil War, which would rend asunder the nation he loved. Abraham Lincoln was elected President of the United States in the fall of 1860, and the Southern Confederacy under the presidency of Jefferson Davis was organized in February 1861. Fort Sumter fell on April 13, 1861, and state after state began to secede from the Union. As Scott witnessed these momentous events, his heart was grieved for the nation.[68]

He did not live to witness the bloodshed and destruction of the War Between the States; yet, he knew it was close at hand. In his mind's eye, he could see the clash of the opposing forces from the North and South. The Union Blue bore the Stars and Stripes into the heat of battle to the tune of the "Battle Hymn of the Republic":

> Mine eyes have seen the glory
> of the coming of the Lord!
> He is trampling out the vintage
> where the grapes of wrath are stored!
> He hath loosed the fateful lightning
> of his terrible swift sword;
> His truth is marching on.
>> Glory! glory! Hallelujah!
>> Glory! glory! Hallelujah!
>> Glory! glory! Hallelujah!
>> His truth is marching on.

On a hill opposite the Union army, he could also hear through the ears of his heart the bugle sound the call to arms and the distant roll of drums. The Confederate Grey proudly carried the Stars and Bars, with the words of "Dixie" echoing through the valley:

> Oh, I wish I was in the land of cotton;
> Old times there are not forgotten;
> Look away! Look away! Look away! Dixieland.
> In Dixieland where I was born
> Early on a frosty morning—
> Look away! Look away! Look away! Dixieland.

While the nation was in the throes of travail and turmoil, in the fall of 1860 Scott wrote an essay entitled "Crisis,"[69] for his myriad friends in both the North and

41

the South, pleading passionately that the Union be preserved. His personal letters to his son, John, indicate the agony he was experiencing over the events of the day. Toward the end of 1860, he wrote:

> I can think of nothing but the sorrows and dangers of my most beloved adopted country. God is witness to my tears and grief. I am cast down, I am afflicted, I am all broken to pieces. My confidence in man is gone. May the Father of mercies show us mercy! Mine eye runneth over with grief. In the Revolution, God gave us a man equal to the occasion; but at this gloomy crisis such a man is wanting; let us look to God, then.[70]

When the war was a certainty, he again wrote to his son, John, in April 1861:

> The fate of Fort Sumter, which you had not heard of when you wrote — which, indeed, occurred subsequently to the date of your letter — will now have reached you. Alas, for my country! Civil war is now most certainly inaugurated, and its termination who can foresee? Who can predict? Twice has the state of things filled my eyes with tears this day. Oh, my country! my country! How I love thee! how I deplore thy present misfortunes.[71]

As the Civil War was beginning, Walter Scott's earthly pilgrimage was ending. He was sixty-four years old, his body spent; he was given to spells of despondency. Yet, looking back over the long years he could find a measure of satisfaction and solace of spirit in the words of the Apostle Paul: "I have fought the good fight, I have finished the race, I have kept the faith" (II Tim. 4:7). He became ill with typhoid pneumonia and died at May's Lick on Tuesday, April 23, 1861. Notices of his death appeared in the leading religious and secular journals of the day. Many tributes were offered in memory of his life, his character and contributions to the church. Alexander Campbell, on hearing of his friend's death, wrote of him as "my most cordial and indefatigable fellow laborer in the origin and progress of the present reformation."[72] Perhaps the most fitting and praiseworthy of these tributes to Walter Scott was given by his biographer, William Baxter:

> In the light of his finished life and labors, it is not an extravagant eulogy to say that he was a man of eminent ability, and that he consecrated all his talents to the service of his Lord and Master; that to his magnificent powers of mind were joined humility, benevolence, and piety; that his errors were few and his virtues many; that his life, labors, and example are a rich legacy to the church of God. His fame will continue to brighten as the years go by, and his memory will long be cherished for the service he did for God and humanity in calling attention to long neglected and almost forgotten truths. Many, very many will be the stars in his crown of rejoicing, and we can not doubt that at the final day his welcome will be: "Well done, good and faithful servant; enter into the joy of thy Lord."[73]

FOOTNOTES

1. See *The Autobiography of Walter Scott: 1796-1861*, ed. and with a Foreword by Roscoe M. Pierson (Lexington, Ky.: Bosworth Memorial Library, The College of the Bible, 1952; reprint, by permission of ed., Cincinnati: Carthage Christian Church, 1970).

2. A.S. Hayden, *Early History of the Disciples in the Western Reserve, Ohio; with Biographical Sketches of the Principal Agents in their Religious Movement* (Cincinnati: Chase & Hall, Publishers, 1875), p. 61.

3. William Baxter, *Life of Elder Walter Scott: With Sketches of his Fellow-Laborers, William Hayden, Adamson Bentley, John Henry, and Others* (Cincinnati: Bosworth, Chase & Hall Publishers, 1874), pp. 29-30.

4. See Librarian of the University of Edinburgh to Dwight E. Stevenson, 24 April 1946, Disciples of Christ Historical Society, Nashville, Tenn.; and Marjorie Robertson, Assistant Librarian, Edinburgh University Library to William A. Gerrard III, 12 October 1979, Disciples of Christ Historical Society, Nashville, Tenn.

5. Winfred Ernest Garrison, *Religion Follows the Frontier: A History of the Disciples of Christ* (New York: Harper, 1931), p. 119, wrote that Scott graduated from the University of Edinburgh in 1818 and came to America almost immediately.

6. Librarian of the University of Edinburgh to Dwight E. Stevenson.

7. Joseph C. Todd, "Moffatt — Birthplace of Walter Scott," *Christian Standard* 73 (January 1938): 53.

8. Dwight E. Stevenson, *Walter Scott: Voice of the Golden Oracle: A Biography* (St. Louis: Christian Board of Publication, 1946), p. 22.

9. *The Autobiography of Walter Scott*, p. 1.

10. Ibid., p. 1.

11. See John W. Neth, Jr., "An Introduction to George Forrester" (B.D. thesis, Butler University, 1951).

12. Hayden, *Early History of the Disciples in the Western Reserve*, pp. 62-63.

13. Stevenson, *Walter Scott: Voice of the Golden Oracle*, p. 27.

14. Walter Scott, *The Messiahship, or Great Demonstration, written for the Union of Christians, on Christian Principles, as plead for in the Current Reformation* (Cincinnati: H.S. Bosworth, 1859), p. 7.

15. *The Evangelist* 6 (January 1838): 286.

16. Winfred Ernest Garrison and Alfred T. DeGroot, *The Disciples of Christ: A History* (St. Louis: Bethany Press, 1964), p. 181.

17. *The Autobiography of Walter Scott*, p. 2.

18. Isaac Errett, *Linsey-Woolsy and Other Addresses* (Cincinnati: The Standard Publishing Company, 1893), p. 319.

19. Baxter, *Life of Elder Walter Scott*, p. 56.

20. Ibid., pp. 60-61.

21. Ibid., p. 73.

22. *The Christian Baptist*, ed. Alexander Campbell, rev. by D.S. Burnet, from the 2nd. ed., with Mr. Campbell's Last Corrections. 7 vols. in 1. (Cincinnati: published by D.S. Burnet, printed by James and Gazlay, 1835).

23. See John Watson Neth, *Walter Scott Speaks — A Handbook of Doctrine* (Berne, Indiana: Economy Printing Concern, 1967), pp. 136-139. Neth has arranged a chronology of Scott's life and family. He was married three times; his first two wives died. He had a total of seven children. See also, *The Autobiography of Walter Scott*, pp. 1-5.

24. The most thorough history of the Mahoning Baptist Associa-

tion is Mary Agnes Monroe Smith, "A History of the Mahoning Baptist Association" (M.A. thesis, West Virginia University, 1943). See also "Printed copy of the minutes of the Mahoning Baptist Association and of the corresponding and circular letters sent to similar associations and member churches, 1821-1827" (Cleveland: Library of the Western Reserve Historical Society); and "Journal of the Mahoning Baptist Association. Minutes of the meetings 1820-1827; Constitution of the Association; and articles of faith of the ten original member churches as well as others which were added in later years" (Hiram, Ohio: Hiram College Library).

25. Stevenson, *Walter Scott: Voice of the Golden Oracle*, p. 47.

26. Hayden, *Early History of the Disciples in the Western Reserve*, p. xiii., has described the location of the Connecticut Western Reserve geographically: "This district of country, also called 'Connecticut Western Reserve,' and 'New Connecticut,' is situated in the northeast part of the state of Ohio. It is bounded on the north by Lake Erie, east by Pennsylvania, south by the 41st parallel of north latitude, and on the west by Sandusky and Seneca counties. . . . The area includes about 3,000,000 acres. It embraces the following counties, viz.: Ashtabula, Trumbull, north part of Mahoning, Lake, Geauga, Portage, Cuyahoga, Summit, Medina, Lorain, Erie, and Huron."

27. Mary Agnes Monroe Smith, "A History of the Mahoning Baptist Association," pp. 36-38.

28. William Warren Sweet, *The Story of Religion in America* (New York: Harper, 1950), p. 207.

29. Mary Agnes Monroe Smith, "A History of the Mahoning Baptist Association," p. 11.

30. See Hayden, *Early History of the Disciples in the Western Reserve*. This is the most thorough treatment of the founding and history of the churches in the Mahoning Baptist Association.

31. Baxter, *Life of Elder Walter Scott*, p. 88. See also Mary Agnes Monroe Smith, "A History of the Mahoning Baptist Association," p. 26.

32. Hayden, *Early History of the Disciples in the Western Reserve*, pp. 27-29.

33. Isaac Errett, "Fifty-Nine Years of History," *Christian Standard* 21 (June 1886): 185.

34. Baxter, *Life of Elder Walter Scott*, pp. 96-101.

35. Ibid., p. 82.

36. Robert Richardson, *Memoirs of Alexander Campbell, Embracing a View of the Origin, Progress, and Principles of the Religious Reformation Which He Advocated*, 2 vols. (Nashville: Gospel Advocate Company, 1956), 2:199.

37. Hayden, *Early History of the Disciples in the Western Reserve*, pp.

57-58. See also "Minutes of the Mahoning Baptist Association," New Lisbon, Ohio, 1827.

38. *The Evangelist* 1 (April 1832): 94

39. Hayden, *Early History of the Disciples in the Western Reserve*, p. 71.

40. Ibid., p. 72.

41. A summary of Scott's New Lisbon sermon was recorded by Baxter, *Life of Elder Walter Scott*, pp. 104-105.

42. Ibid., pp. 106-108. These steps, as Scott later preached them, became popularly known as the "five-finger exercise." Sometimes "resurrection" or "eternal life" was added as the sixth point in the formula.

43. For a detailed account of Scott's first year as Evangelist for the Mahoning Baptist Association, see Baxter, *Life of Elder Walter Scott*, pp. 109-193, and Hayden, *Early History of the Disciples in the Western Reserve*, pp. 76-160.

44. Baxter, *Life of Elder Walter Scott*, pp. 158-159.

45. Ibid., pp. 188-193.

46. Hayden, *Early History of the Disciples in the Western Reserve*, pp. 161-174. See also *The Autobiography of Walter Scott*, p. 5.

47. Baxter, *Life of Elder Walter Scott*, p. 216.

48. Ibid., pp. 216-217.

49. Ibid., pp. 216-217.

50. See William Garrett West, *Barton Warren Stone: Early American Advocate of Christian Unity* (Nashville: Disciples of Christ Historical Society, 1954.

51. Walter Scott, *A Discourse on the Holy Spirit*, 2nd. ed., enl. and imp. (Bethany, Va.: printed by Alexander Campbell, 1831).

52. The exception to this was in 1837 when the name of *The Evangelist* was changed to *The Christian*, and Scott co-edited it with John T. Johnson at Georgetown, Kentucky. See John T. Johnson and Walter Scott, eds., *The Christian, A Monthly Publication, devoted to the Union of Protestants upon the Foundation of the Original Gospel and the Apostolic Order of the Primitive Church*, vol. 1 (Georgetown, Ky.: printed by Stuart & Stark, Main-st., 1837).

53. Walter Scott, *The Gospel Restored. A Discourse of the True Gospel of Jesus Christ, in Which the Facts, Principles, Duties, and Privileges of Christianity are Arranged, Defined, and Discussed, and the Gospel in its Various Parts Shewn to be Adapted to the Nature and Necessities of Man in His Present Condition. The Evangelist for the Current Year* (Cincinnati: printed by O.H. Donogh, 1836).

54. See Dwight E. Stevenson, "The Bacon College Story: 1836-1865," *The College of the Bible Quarterly* 29 (October 1962): 1-56.

55. Walter Scott, "United States System: An Address," *The College*

of the Bible Quarterly 23 (April 1946): 4-44.

56. Stevenson, "The Bacon College Story," p. 12.

57. Walter Scott, "Personal Notebook, 1836-1847" (Library of Lexington Theological Seminary, Lexington, Kentucky).

58. Stevenson, *Walter Scott: Voice of the Golden Oracle*, p. 165.

59. From 1834-1844, it was variously called *The Evangelist of the True Gospel* and *The Carthage Evangelist*.

60. *The Protestant Unionist* was published in Pittsburgh and Cincinnati. Robert H. Forrester and later T.J. Melish served as co-editors with Scott.

61. Garrison, *Religion Follows the Frontier*, p. 186.

62. See Walter Small, "May's Lick Church Record," Library of Lexington Theological Seminary, Lexington, Kentucky.

63. Stevenson, *Walter Scott: Voice of the Golden Oracle*, pp. 201-203.

64. Walter Scott, *To Themelion:The Union of Christians, on Christian Principles* (Cincinnati: C.A. Morgan & Co., 1852).

65. Walter Scott, *He Nekrosis, or The Death of Christ. Written for the Recovery of the Church from Sects* (Cincinnati: C.A. Morgan & Co., 1853).

66. Stevenson, *Walter Scott: Voice of the Golden Oracle*, pp. 207-209.

67. Small, "May's Lick Church Record."

68. Stevenson, *Walter Scott: Voice of the Golden Oracle*, pp. 207-209.

69. See Baxter, *Life of Elder Walter Scott*, pp. 443-440, for several introductory pages of the essay. There are no extant copies of the whole essay.

70. Ibid., p. 441.

71. Ibid., p. 445.

72. *The Millennial Harbinger* (1861): 296.

73. Baxter, *Life of Elder Walter Scott*, pp. 449-450.

CHAPTER TWO

THE SKELETON
AND THE FLESH

The writer descended of religious ancestors, was of the family of "The Scotts of Thirstane," ... Being invited hither by his Uncle George Innes, who had been thirty years in the service of the United States, he arrived in N York, Ship Glenthorn, Stilman Captain, from Greenock 7th July 1818.

The Autobiography of Walter Scott: 1796-1861, p. 1.

Among the Christian governments of the old world ... none unfurls a broader and more glorious banner than Great Britain.... In Great Britain and the United States we have before us, one in the new and one in the old world, the most illustrious proofs that the Messiah who was to come is come, and that the better order of things indicated in the prophets is inaugurated in these two governments at least.

Walter Scott, *The Messiahship*, pp. 297-298.

Walter Scott emigrated from Scotland to America in 1818, and as far as is known never returned to his motherland. Though he left Scotland, Scotland never left him! It remained a part of him for the rest of his life. How often throughout the course of his years in America did his mind drift back to the days of yore in Scotland and the cherished memories it held. He could almost see the beautiful Highlands of Scotland and the Highlanders with their checkered plaids, kilts, and tam-o'-shanters. How he loved to hear the sound of the bagpipes off in the distance!

He remembered his days in Edinburgh and the old Scottish custom of "first foot." According to this custom, a house would be blessed by the one who put the "first foot" across the threshold after the clock struck twelve at midnight on December 31. He recalled the time he was the "first foot" over the door of a friend. Later in America he often wondered whether prosperity had followed his friend and sunshine had fallen on the home. He hoped it had!

There was his rearing in a Scottish home, where a deep religious faith was instilled in him. His parents brought him up as a member of the Presbyterian Kirk (Church) of Scotland. He loved the church, embraced its beliefs early in life, and studied its history at the University of Edinburgh. He was well-read in the heroic struggles of the young Scottish reformer, John Knox, and how he openly and successfully challenged the Roman Catholic queen, Mary Stuart, better known as Mary, "Queen of Scots." A bold John Knox had insisted that the Scottish Church must return to the New Testament and purge its house of all beliefs and practices not clearly enjoined in Scripture. The Reformation cause won the day there. Largely through the efforts of Knox, the Presbyterian Kirk of Scotland came into being.

In his home church Walter Scott learned almost by heart "The Westminster Confession of Faith," the church's official creed, and especially the opening section on Scripture:

> The authority of the Holy Scripture . . . dependeth not on the testimony of any man or Church; but wholly upon God (who is truth itself) the author thereof. . . . Nothing is at any time to be added whether by new revelations of the Spirit or traditions of men. . . . The Church is finally to appear to them. . . . The infallible rule of interpretation of Scripture is the Scripture itself . . . .

Throughout his life Scott never departed from this high view of the central importance of the Scriptures, a truth he learned early in life. As with John Knox, Walter Scott had drunk deeply from the spirit of the Holy Scriptures. Yes, though he left Scotland, Scotland never left him!

Implicit in the church of his youth was the strong belief that the church should be free from state control and free to serve God as revealed in Scripture. In the world there are many distinctions of rank and class, but all stand before God on an equal footing. This was for a long time expressed in a meaningful way in the Scottish Church custom of celebrating the Lord's Supper at a long table. Around this table all sat as a family in complete equality, with Christ as Host seated at the head. A favorite slogan among the Scottish Presbyterians was "The Crown Rights of the Redeemer," meaning by this that the Lordship of Christ in the church is preeminent over all other human authorities.

This heritage of faith from his youth remained with him the rest of his life, and he never lost his distinct Scottish accent. When preaching the Word, he held the audiences spellbound and captivated not only with what he said, but also by the way he spoke with such a clear, resonant voice. Who could miss his distinctive pronunciation, marked by a tongue-tip trill for the sound of "r." A worshipper was often heard to say to another, "Listen to him speak and that accent. Where did he come from? He doesn't talk like we do." The other would answer, "I believe he must be from Scotland."

On more than one occasion, when he was introduced, someone would say, "Walter Scott! Are you Walter Scott, the poet? Are you the one who wrote 'The Lay of the Last Minstrel,' 'Ivanhoe,' and 'The Lady of the Lake'? These are my favorites."

He responded with a broad smile. "Oh, no, I am not 'that' Walter Scott. But we are of the same Scott Clan. The poet is of the House of Hardin, and I belong to the House of Thirstane. I am proud to be in his clan. We both went to Edinburgh University, but he was there about twenty years before me. I was often asked by my fellow students if I were kin to him. There were a lot of us Walter Scotts at the University then." Again, he left Scotland, but Scotland never left him! Cherished memories from the motherland were fresh in his mind until the snow fell gently on his grave.

Walter Scott was born and raised in Scotland, but he was equally proud to be British and part of the Commonwealth. Although America was his future home, and he gave his allegiance to the Stars and Stripes, in his heart he continued to revere the British Union Jack. So strong were his feelings about Great Britain that he often referred to it as a "Messianic nation" with a destiny along with the United States of spreading the gospel to the four corners of the world. Not only was Scotland and the British Isles his homeland and full of memories, but it was also important to him in another more significant way. It was the British — the English, the Irish, and especially the Scotch — who influenced him and helped shape the background for his thought in his early years.

There were the Scotsmen — George Forrester, John Glas, Robert Sandeman, James A. Haldane and Robert Haldane (the Scottish Independents). Important also were Thomas Campbell and Alexander Campbell, Alexander himself studying for a year at the University of Glasgow. Significant were two Englishmen, Francis Bacon and John Locke, in the English Enlightenment. Besides these persons and movements there were a number of prominent Scottish and English biblical scholars whom he read and studied. These were the persons who stood to the immediate background and influenced Scott's thinking. They formed the skeleton for the flesh and muscles of the gospel as he understood it. To these persons and movements and the way they impacted Scott's thinking we now turn.

George Forrester

When Walter Scott knocked on the door of George Forrester's home in Pittsburgh and introduced himself, he met a man who would be a significant influence in his life.[1] As his mentor, Forrester introduced his fellow countryman to a new conception of the Christian faith and church order that was at variance with his Presbyterian upbringing in the Church of Scotland. Theologically the Church of Scotland was Calvinistic and adhered to "The Westminster Confession of Faith," the standard creedal expression of the Presbyterians. Scott soon found to his pleasure that the Haldanean congregation which Forrester pastored was different. The Haldanes believed that one must return to Primitive Christianity and the Scriptures as the sole authority. George Forrester quickened in Scott a desire to study the Scriptures in a new way. He was thereby instrumental in giving new direction to his thinking by posing the conception of the Scriptures as authoritative in all matters of faith and church life. Together they spent many hours in intensive Bible study, and through this Scott came to a new appreciation of the centrality of the Scriptures. His relationship with Forrester and the Haldanes caused him to question and rethink his views of the Church of Scotland, its Calvinistic theological orientation, and creedal formulation. This fresh, new approach to the study of Scripture was for Scott like turning a "Copernican corner." Baxter has expressed what this meant at this juncture in his life.

> Mr. Scott now felt that he had discovered the true theology; the Bible had for him a meaning that it never had before; . . . to devoutly study it in order to reach its meaning, was to put himself in possession of the mind and will of God. It was no longer a repository of texts, from which to draw proofs of doctrines of modern or

ancient origin, which could not be expressed in the words of Scripture, but a revelation, an unveiling of the will of God — the gospel was a message, and to believe and obey that message was to be a Christian.[2]

Through his study of the Scriptures, Scott began to adopt a different conception of the mode of baptism. Working in the original Greek, Scott made a study of all references in the New Testament to baptism. He concluded that baptism was not administered by sprinkling or pouring. In abandoning infant baptism, he subscribed to the idea that the New Testament mode of baptism is immersion.[3] Thus, George Forrester was the one who guided Scott in arriving at this view of baptism. This would become one of the cardinal tenets of the Reformers and the Disciples of Christ movement.

As Scott continued to study, he searched for an understanding of the essential message of the Scriptures. The idea that there was one clear, authoritative plan of salvation began to engross his attention. In his study with Forrester, Scott did not come to any new discovery. Rather, he saw in the Bible an orderliness and a relationship between various ideas that he believed had been lost to the church for centuries. Scott thought that one could read and study, believe and obey the Scriptures apart from the mysterious, inner operation of the Holy Spirit as expressed in the Calvinistic view of conversion. A new understanding of the Christian faith and a different conception of conversion were developing in his mind. Central among these was the scriptural injunction that a profession of faith by the individual must precede baptism. This understanding was at variance with that of the Methodists and Presbyterians who practiced infant baptism.[4]

This conception of faith and baptism was not the fully developed plan of salvation that Scott would later set forth in his preaching and writing, but the first steps toward its formulation were taken during these years. Scott was in the process of developing a carefully reasoned approach to the Scriptures and a model of conversion that was an alternative to the Calvinistic mode prevalent in his day. As he wrestled with these vital issues of faith that were fermenting in his mind, George Forrester was a significant influence, and his guiding hand was on Scott's shoulder.

The Scottish Independents

George Forrester was principally responsible for mediating the ideas of the Scottish Independents to Scott. After Forrester's death, he had access to his library which contained many of their writings. He spent many evening hours pouring through these volumes. Because of this direct connection, an overview of the Scottish Independents is important for understanding Scott.

During the eighteenth century in Great Britain, there arose several movements whose aim was a restoration of Primitive Christianity.[5] None of these movements was able to gain a very large following, but they did establish some churches. The leaders who were instrumental in launching these movements were daring, independent spirits who insisted that the church of their day was in need of reforming. Among the more prominent of these Scottish innovators were John Glas, Robert Sandeman, and James A. and Robert Haldane.[6] The writings of these Scottish Independents were widely read in Great Britain and America during the eighteenth and nineteenth centuries.

Glas and Sandeman

John Glas[7] was a Presbyterian minister in the Church of Scotland. Around 1728, Glas broke with the Church of Scotland over the issue of the connection between the church and state. He made a distinction between the Old and New Testaments on church-state relations. In the Old Testament, according to Glas, the church and state were identical, whereas the New Testament church was solely a spiritual entity having no connection with the state. With this biblical precedent, Glas rejected the "National Covenant" in Scotland and the conception of an established church whereby the nation was bound to God through a particular church. Further, Glas rejected the idea of synods or other law-making bodies that had ecclesiastical authority to prescribe the standard doctrine for the church.

Breaking away from the Church of Scotland, Glas organized his own church. In ordering the affairs of his church on matters of faith, worship, and doctrine, Glas used the New Testament and the primitive Christian community as a guide. His assumption was that the New Testament presented an explicit blueprint and authorized plan for the organization and life of the church. Among the more prominent features of his church were the weekly observance of the Lord's Supper (Acts 20:6-8) and a plurality of elders (Acts 15:2,22). Since Glas believed that the locus of authority is with the elders, leadership by the laity in his church was stressed. Laymen as well as ordained ministers were to participate in the conduct of public worship. According to Glas, the church is comprised of individuals who have separated from the world and organized into autonomous local congregations controlled by the elders.

John Glas was soon joined by his son-in-law, Robert Sandeman. Vigorously advocating the principles of Glas, Robert Sandeman gave a positive thrust to the movement. Through the combined efforts of Glas and Sandeman, there arose a number of churches variously called "Glasites" or "Sandemanians." In all there were probably no more than twenty to thirty of these churches in England and Scotland. In America in the mid-eighteenth century, the movement was confined to the New England states. Some of the churches formed here were in Boston, Mass.; Portsmouth, N.H.; and Danbury, Conn. The basic idea of Sandeman, as with Glas, was the restoration of the primitive Christian church and a return to the New Testament for the principles of church organization and faith. Since the restoration motif was the central concern of Glas and Sandeman, there was no consideration given to the idea of Christian union among the various factions of the church in Great Britain and America. Sandeman was a theological thinker and writer of no mean ability, and his writings were widely read and discussed in Great Britain and America.[8]

One of the central ideas Sandeman set forth was on the nature of faith. He expressed this in a pronounced way in his polemic against James Hervey. Hervey[9] viewed faith as the effect of regenerating or enabling grace upon the heart of the believer. In true Calvinistic fashion, Hervey believed that the individual cannot in and of himself believe until he is regenerated. A person can repent and mourn the sinful state inherited from Adam, but must wait for the miracle of enabling grace in order to have faith. Hervey placed emphasis upon the emotional experience, which he called the "sense of adoption," and this emotional state was identified with the gift of saving faith. In his scheme, faith was principally a feeling state rather than a rational act on the part of the human intellect. For Hervey, faith was at the end of the whole process of conversion and not at the beginning.

Sandeman's reply to Hervey was his *Letters on Theron and Aspasio. Addressed to the Author.* In this work, Sandeman's basic endeavor was to delineate the conception of faith as belief in testimony, followed by repentance in the order of salvation. According to Sandeman, every person has the capacity to believe the gospel and respond to its commands concerning salvation. The truths of God regarding salvation, which have been set forth in the Scriptures, are intelligible to the individual. Sandeman's major point was that the sinful person can weigh the evidences of Scripture concerning revelation and the salvation of humankind and accept its truths. Faith, then, is accepting these evidences and is an act of the human intellect. Sandeman, however, was a Calvinist and affirmed that, although all persons have the capacity to believe the evidences in Scripture, only those who had been elected by God can perform the rational act of believing. God gives the Holy Spirit to the elect, thus enabling them to believe. Sandeman, then, placed faith first in the process of salvation, to be followed by repentance. Changes in the heart and feelings, which give the individual the assurances of salvation, are the effect of faith. As opposed to this, Hervey identified one's feeling state with faith.

The churches formed by Glas and Sandeman practiced infant baptism and viewed it as the seal of the new covenant, analogous to the Old Testament rite of circumcision. Some of the associates of Glas and Sandeman, however, adopted the position of baptism of believers by immersion. One of the more prominent leaders advocating the immersionist position was Archibald McLean. He had left the Presbyterian Church of Scotland in 1762 to join with the Glas-Sandeman movement. After three years McLean separated from them and, along with his followers, founded what was called the "Scotch Baptists." McLean and his associates continued to adhere to the basic ideas of Glas and Sandeman, with the exception of baptism by immersion, which was one of their central tenets.

The position of the Scotch Baptists on the subject of baptism was expressed in the pamphlet, *On Baptism*,[10] by Henry Errett in New York City. According to Errett's interpretation of the New Testament passages relating to the subject, baptism was to be administered by immersion of believers. Thereby, he rejected the practice of baptizing infants. The purpose of baptism was for the remission of sins through the death of Jesus Christ and was therefore connected with salvation; it was called

"the bath of regeneration." Errett also emphasized the
Pauline idea of baptism as a burial with Jesus Christ
and being raised with Him to a newness of life (Rom.
6:2-11). Errett most clearly enunciated the meaning of
baptism when he wrote:

> If the language employed respecting it, in many of the
> passages, were to be taken literally, it would import,
> that "remission of sins" is to be obtained by baptism;
> that an "escape from the wrath to come" is effected in
> baptism; that "men are born the children of God" by
> baptism; that "salvation" is connected with baptism;
> that men "wash away their sins" by baptism; that men
> become "dead to sin and alive to God," by baptism; that
> the Church of God is "sanctified and cleansed" by bap-
> tism; that men are "regenerated" by baptism; and that
> the "answer of a good conscience" is obtained by bap-
> tism. All these things, if all the passages before us were
> construed literally, would be ascribed to baptism. And it
> was a literal construction of these passages which led
> professed Christians, in the early ages, to believe that
> baptism was necessary to salvation.[11]

The Haldanes

A movement in certain ways similar to that of Glas
and Sandeman was begun by James Alexander Haldane
and his brother Robert Haldane, two wealthy laymen in
the Church of Scotland.[12] The Haldanes had become dis-
satisfied with the Church of Scotland because of its connection with the state and also because they saw the
church doing very little to preach the gospel to those
who were in need of it. They viewed the church as a
sterile, formal institution; many of the clergy were too
worldly-minded.

While they were still members of the Church of Scotland, they gave their time and money to promote evangelistic revivals in Scotland, build tabernacles in Edinburgh and Glasgow, and organize Sunday Schools. The Haldanes encouraged preaching by laymen and financed institutes for the training of young men from poor families to preach the gospel. In their concern for spreading the gospel, the Haldanes brought the prominent English evangelist, Rowland Hill, from London to conduct preaching missions in Scotland and Ireland. In 1797, James A. Haldane organized the Society for Propagating the Gospel at Home, an evangelistic agency.

The Haldanes, having become further disenchanted with the Church of Scotland, broke with it in January 1799. They organized their own independent congregation in Edinburgh, and on February 3, 1799 James A. Haldane became its minister and continued his work there for fifty years. In order to train young men for the ministry, a seminary was established in Glasgow and underwritten financially by Robert Haldane. The Haldane seminary at Glasgow, which was headed by Greville Ewing, trained over three hundred ministers during the next ten years. Haldane churches soon sprang up in Great Britain and America. There were not a large number of these congregations, but they were a recognized religious movement, and the writings of the Haldanes were widely read and influential. The basic thrust of the movement begun by the Haldanes was to restore the New Testament church, preach the gospel for the conversion of sinners, and promote holiness in the lives of believers. All creedal formulations were excluded from their theology and worship.

In 1805, James A. Haldane published his major work, *A View of the Social Worship and Ordinances Observed by the First Christians*.[13] In this writing, Haldane delineated the restorationist view concerning the church. His position was that the New Testament gave instructions concerning the worship, faith, and organization of the church and the conduct of Christians. The present-day church must return to Primitive Christianity in order to be reformed and restored to what it was intended to be. Haldane argued for infant baptism as the practice of the apostles in the Early Church. Two years after the publication of this work, however, the Haldanes became convinced that New Testament baptism was by immersion. In so doing, they abandoned their practice of infant baptism and were themselves baptized by immersion.

Their restorationism entailed a congregational form of church government, in which local churches were autonomous and independent of presbyteries, synods, or other ecclesiastical authorities. The Lord's Supper was observed every week at their services of worship, but only their own members were able to partake. In conjunction with the Lord's Supper, members also partook of a common meal. In their endeavor to restore Primitive Christianity and reform the church of their day, the Haldane movement was characterized by a thoroughly literal interpretation of the Scriptures. The New Testament must be followed in all matters pertaining to the faith and life of the church. Thus, they saluted one another with a "holy kiss" (Rom. 16:16), engaged in foot washing (John 13:14), and took a weekly collection for the poor (I Cor. 16:2).

As with the Glas-Sandeman movement, the Haldanes

showed no interest in Christian union. Their prime concern was to be right by conforming to the New Testament. They had little or no interest in uniting with other Christian bodies whom they considered to be in error.

Similarities exist between the Scottish Independents and Scott's thinking on several key issues of faith. Thus, the Scottish Independents influenced him and formed a significant part of his philosophical and theological heritage.

First, the idea of the restoration of Primitive Christianity as advocated by Glas and Sandeman and the Haldanes was a major influence on Scott's thinking. Although Scott was concerned with the restorationist motif, his emphasis was on recovering the Ancient Gospel and the message of the Early Church more so than on its worship and organization. Scott believed that Alexander Campbell had recovered the Ancient Order of the church in its essential features, and with Campbell he was in accord. Second, in close connection with the restorationist motif was the idea of the Scottish Independents that the Scriptures should be the sole guide in all matters of faith and church order, all creeds being excluded. The principal thrust of Scott's theology was a delineation of the Christian faith on the basis of the Scriptures alone, and in this he was profoundly influenced by the Scottish Independents. Third, Sandeman's idea that faith was a rational act of believing the evidences in the Scriptures and that repentance followed faith exerted a lasting influence on Scott's thinking. In the steps of salvation Scott formulated, one of the key conceptions was this rational interpretation of faith, followed by repentance and baptism. Fourth, the ideas of the Scotch Baptists and the Haldanes concerning baptism by immersion for the remission of sins had an impact on Scott's thought in his formative years. It was largely due to the Scottish Independents that Scott abandoned the practice of infant baptism and adopted the immersionist position.

The English Enlightenment

One of the more prominent modern intellectual movements shaping the thought of Scott was the Enlightenment in England. His writings show a broad knowledge of and familiarity with the major Enlightenment philosophers and scientists; however, his philosophical and theological orientation was shaped principally by Francis Bacon, John Locke, and certain English and Scottish biblical scholars representative of Enlightenment hermeneutics.

Francis Bacon and the Baconian Heritage

One of the leading philosophers of the English Enlightenment was Francis Bacon.[14] In his theological writings, Scott referred to Bacon numerous times. His inaugural address, *United States System*, given in 1837 at Bacon College was an extended treatment of Bacon's principal work, *Novum Organon*.[15] In the *United States System*, Scott endeavored to show that Bacon had formulated the inductive methodology in science, going from particulars to the general. Bacon gave a set of rules for investigating scientific data, and taught the proper method of studying the various sciences so as to arrive at "the ultimate law of nature in the particular case."[16]

Scott saw a whole new approach to science, philosophy, and other areas of human endeavor brought into being by the Baconian philosophy. Bacon was a master genius, a "philosopher who may be regarded as the morning star of that illustrious day which has since broken out upon mankind."[17] Scott perceived himself as a participant in this new era, the Enlightenment, and his theology was set within the framework of the world perspective brought about by Bacon and the inductive method.

The inductive method, going from particulars to the general, was employed especially by Enlightenment thinkers in England and Scotland in their search for the universal or original in all branches of learning.[18] In the religious realm, one can see in many thinkers this Enlightenment concern to discover the universal law, principle, or source beneath the specific historical manifestations of religion. In the attempt to discern the real essence of Christianity, the Bible was viewed by many as the universal source of truth; in the particulars of the biblical texts one could discern the presence of universal truths. For these thinkers, the fundamental principles of the Christian faith were contained in the Bible, and these religious truths were to be discovered by critical biblical study. Some schools of eighteenth century biblical hermeneutics were built on the Baconian inductive methodology. Also, many of the eighteenth century restoration movements in Great Britain came into being and were influenced to a large extent by the intellectual climate of the Enlightenment and Baconian induction.

The Enlightenment idea of searching for the universal found expression also in the emphasis on an "original state of nature" or "Golden Age," as in Hobbes, Butler, and Locke. A return to a Golden Age or idealized age in the past was generally applied in an historical sense by Enlightenment thinkers. One needed to eliminate the accretions of history and return to a simple, unadulterated age in the past. Humanity in the natural state before being corrupted could be found in the Golden Age.

Enlightenment thinking in the eighteenth century entailed not only returning to a Golden Age in the past but also an optimistic look toward the future and a glorious new age. This hope-oriented and optimistic perspective insisted that progress was being made towards the betterment of the whole human race and society. The Enlightenment thinkers gave special consideration to the education of persons to their fullest potential. Education had as its purpose the progress and perfection of humankind religiously, morally, socially, and intellectually. Through education all superstition and ignorance would be eliminated, thereby aiding in bringing in a glorious future bright with promise. This progressive optimism and hope for a new age continued into the nineteenth century and was a dominant force during the time of Campbell and Scott.

A significant feature of the Enlightenment was the conception of the individual as an autonomous being endowed with the capacity to reason. Enlightenment thinking was usually characterized by a turning away from externally imposed authority and church dogmas.

In this revolt against authoritarianism, there was the emergence of the individual who could reason and be the arbiter of truth and his own actions. In the English Enlightenment, the model for reason was the inductive, experimental reason of Bacon and Locke. Eighteenth century thought was characterized by a new look at and interest in the observable phenomena of nature and those truths that could be derived from nature by the unaided human reason. The autonomous individual was able to examine the facts of experience as they were presented, use his critical faculties, and draw valid conclusions.

The inductive method of Bacon and the general tenor of English Enlightenment thought was influential for Scott's theology in four particular areas. First, the conception of searching for the universal principle and returning to a Golden Age in the past, so characteristic of Enlightenment thought, was determinative in Scott's thinking. One sees this influence reflected in his endeavor to restore the Ancient Gospel and return to the New Testament as sole authority. In Scott's thinking, the gospel had been distorted and for all practical purposes lost through nineteen centuries of Christian history. One must remove all of these distortions and accretions and return to the gospel as found in the New Testament.

Second, the inductive method of Bacon, proceeding from particulars to the general, was determinative in Scott's approach to interpreting the Scriptures. Every text contained in the Scriptures was regarded as a particular to be examined critically. These scriptural passages were to be studied historically and grammatically in order to ascertain the precise meaning of the words and concepts involved. From a careful inductive examination of a large number of particular words and texts, one could arrive at the general truth or essential principle of faith as expressed in the Scriptures. Scott employed this method in his attempt to understand the meaning of baptism, miracles, and prophecy.

Third, Scott was influenced by the Enlightenment conceptions of intellectual progress through education,[19] optimism for the future, and a new age to come. These Enlightenment ideas, strongly prevalent in nineteenth century America, formed the philosophical framework and interpretation of history that significantly shaped his postmillennialism. Scott saw that the restoration of the Ancient Gospel was a necessary precursor to the reunification of the church. This unified church would preach the gospel, and Christianity would spread from America to the whole world. There would be a steady progress of humankind and society, and the millennial age would arrive. In his latter years, Scott advocated this postmillennial perspective, the one thousand years of peace and prosperity prior to the Second Coming of Christ.

Fourth, the Enlightenment conception of the autonomous individual as a being endowed with reason was a pronounced feature in Scott's thought. Unaided by the supernatural influence of the Holy Spirit as in orthodox Calvinism, one could read the Scriptures, weigh the evidences, and make the decision in faith that Jesus Christ is the Messiah and Son of God. One of the cornerstones of Scott's formulation of the Ancient Gospel was his conception of the autonomous individual who had the ability to believe and repent. In this sense, for Scott one's destiny was in one's own hands.

John Locke

Within the Baconian heritage and the Enlightenment in England, one of the towering figures was John Locke.[20] Locke exerted a profound influence on Scott, as is evidenced by the references to him in his theological writings. Especially important for Scott were Locke's *The Reasonableness of Christianity*[21] and some of the epistemological principles laid out by him in *An Essay Concerning Human Understanding*.[22] For the most part, however, Scott modeled his interpretation of the Christian faith on the basis of Locke's ideas in *The Reasonableness of Christianity*.

According to Locke, Christianity is a revelation from God, but it is not out of accord with reason. The essential truths of the Christian faith as taught by Christ and the apostles could not have originated solely in the human mind, but once they are disclosed, the mind is able to grasp them and find them reasonable.[23] Authority within Christianity is not centered in creeds, church councils, or the myriad dogmas that have been formulated in the church. The Scriptures, which are to be interpreted by human reason, are the central authority, and contain the essential truths of the faith.

For Locke, Christianity is a religion centering on the redemption and restoration of all humankind through Jesus Christ. However, the presupposition upon which this rests is the fall of Adam, which Locke interpreted in

an historical sense.[24] Adam, living in paradise, was in a
state of bliss and immortality. When Adam sinned
through disobedience to the commands of God, he lost
this paradise of bliss and immortality and was thereby
turned out of the Garden. The result of Adam's sin for
himself and all humankind was that death entered in,
and by this Locke meant death of the physical body. All
of Adam's posterity have been born out of paradise and
are mortal, with the result that all should experience
death. Although all died in Adam, Locke maintained
that no one is punished for sins except one's own.
Therefore, he rejected the idea of original sin and inherited guilt transmitted to all humankind in a Calvinistic
sense.

In his understanding of the process of salvation,
Locke employed the biblical idea of the covenants, particularly the covenant with Abraham and the new
covenant of grace in Jesus Christ. In order to enter into
the covenant of grace, certain conditions were to be fulfilled:

> An union of faith, repentance, and obedience, is indis-
> pensable for the formation of a sufficient number of sub-
> jects proper for the kingdom of the Messiah; . . . These
> two, faith and repentance; (that is, believing Jesus to be
> the Messiah, and a good life,) are the indispensable con-
> ditions of the new covenant; to be performed by all
> those who would obtain eternal life.[25]

This was the law of the kingdom,[26] and was the meaning of justification by faith. Included, also, in the affirmation of Jesus as the Messiah were what Locke called
the "concomitant articles of his resurrection, rule, and
coming again to judge the world,"[27] belief in which

were required in order to be justified. Locke based his rational interpretation of Christianity upon the idea that revealed truth was propositional,[28] that is, one believed the proposition that Jesus is the Messiah on the basis of evidences presented in the Scriptures. Faith, then, meant giving assent to revealed propositions and accepting the truths Christ taught. The evidences that established these truths about Christ and the Christian faith were of three kinds: miracles, fulfillment of Old Testament prophecies, and the testimony of the apostles in their preaching the gospel after the resurrection.[29]

The essential principles of Christianity, as expressed by Locke in *The Reasonableness of Christianity*, were adopted by Scott and provided to a large extent the framework for his understanding of the Christian faith. Scott appropriated Locke's theory of knowledge in his contention that there are no innate ideas, but that our knowledge comes from sensation and reflection.[30] He also followed Locke's understanding of the nature of religious knowledge and his threefold classification of truths according to reason, above reason, and contrary to reason. For Scott, the Christian faith entails a revelation of truths that are above reason, but they are not contrary to reason.[31]

Locke's influence on Scott is evident in his understanding of Adam and the fall. For Scott, as well as for Locke, Adam's fall was due to his disobedience to the divine commands, resulting in his expulsion from the Garden, a loss of bliss and immortality, and death coming to all humankind. In his development of the three states of humanity (natural, preternatural, and respite), Scott adopted Locke's principles of knowledge.[32] His anthropology was fashioned after Locke's theory that we are dependent upon sensory experience for all of our knowledge, including knowledge of God. Scott modeled his understanding of the Christian faith on the basis of the fall of Adam and the necessity for the restoration of humankind through Jesus Christ. In his conception of the history of salvation, Scott followed Locke in appropriating the idea of the covenants; however, Scott developed the view of a succession of covenants in the Old Testament, culminating in the new covenant in Jesus Christ.

Following Locke, Scott conceived religious truth to be primarily propositional in nature, the central core of the Christian faith being an assent to the proposition that Jesus Christ is the Messiah. Scott called this the "Golden Oracle" and the "Creed of Christianity."[33] Around this belief, all other faith statements revolved. Scott followed Locke in stressing the centrality of faith and repentance, although Scott went beyond Locke in his conception of baptism for the remission of sins and the six steps in the process of salvation. The influence of Locke's rationalistic approach to Christianity is especially pronounced in Scott's conception of the evidences in Scripture for the claim that Jesus Christ is the Messiah. Scott appropriated Locke's idea of miracles and prophecies to substantiate this truth; however, he expanded Locke's idea of miracles to include the miracles Christ performed and those performed on Him.[34]

Not only was Scott in accord with Locke in the view that the New Testament was the sole authority, but he also advocated Locke's concept of the authority of Christ Himself. For Scott and Locke, once the messiahship of Christ was established on the basis of the evidences in the Scriptures, all that he said was authoritative and was to be accepted as revealed truth and obeyed by the individual.

English and Scottish Biblical Interpreters: The Grammatico-Historical Method

In addition to the impact of Bacon and Locke on Scott's thinking was the influence of English and Scottish Enlightenment hermeneutics. Scott's approach to the interpretation of the Scriptures was shaped by some of the prominent eighteenth and nineteenth century biblical scholars in England and Scotland, in particular those whose interpretive principles were in accord with the grammatico-historical method.[35] This method was also very popular and was widely used during the nineteenth century in America, where one of its leading proponents was Moses Stuart at Andover Seminary.

The grammatico-historical method of interpretation of the Scriptures, which had its rootage in Baconian induction, was based on the assumption that one could gain the proper meaning of a biblical text by understanding its grammatical or literary and historical context.[36] Important to this approach was the use of general rules of interpretation that were to be followed in order to understand correctly a passage.[37]

The Bible was to be interpreted by the same rules that guided the interpretation of ancient writings on other subjects. Biblical language could be understood in the same way as the language of other ancient texts. One should seek to discern the author's style of composition, design, and scope of writing. The attempt should be made to put oneself in the condition of the original hearer and recapture the ideas as they were directed to him. In order to accomplish this task of interpreting the biblical writings accurately, the advocates of the grammatico-historical method stressed only the necessity of understanding the grammatical context and historical circumstances. They emphasized seeing a word in its particular context, noting how it was used in other passages, and what meanings it might have in these different instances. The meaning of a word or passage of Scripture was to be determined by its context. Studying the growth of the language aided one in gaining clarity on the etymology of a word. Classical writers and the church fathers should be consulted regarding these grammatical or literary considerations.

Equally important for these interpreters was an understanding of the historical circumstances surrounding the production and reception of the writing. A knowledge of the times and the attendant circumstances was deemed necessary to discern accurately the historical context. In essence, the endeavor should be made to understand the total historical situation in which the words of the text were written and make these clear to the present day reader so that one might hear the biblical message as it was originally heard in the first century.

By having access to the library of his late friend, George Forrester,[38] Scott introduced himself to some of the writings of prominent biblical scholars of the eighteenth and nineteenth century who employed the grammatico-historical method in their interpretation of the Scriptures. Those whom he noted and their particular works were *A Harmony of the Four Gospels*[39] and *The Apostolic Epistles*[40] by James McKnight; *On the Epistles*[41] by George Benson; *The Four Gospels*[42] by George Campbell; *Harmony of the Four Evangelists*[43] by William Newcome; and the *Notes*[44] by Sir Norton Knatchbull. Scott also made references to three other biblical scholars whose works he knew: Joseph Lomas Towers.[45] William Warburton,[46] and Sir Isaac Newton.[47]

In his major theological writings, *The Gospel Restored* and *The Messiahship*, Scott cited these writers numerous times and gave their translations and comments on selected passages of Scripture. Scott employed in his interpretation of the Scriptures, and especially in his endeavors to restore the Ancient Gospel in its original setting, the grammatico-historical method that had been advocated by these scholars. He even had plans to publish a major work on the New Testament in which he would draw heavily from these commentators. Many of these same scholars to whom Scott referred were also cited by Alexander Campbell.[48]

Thomas and Alexander Campbell

The first meeting between Walter Scott and Alexander Campbell in the winter of 1821-1822 was the beginning of a friendship lasting for forty years. They were attracted to each other by a mutuality of interests and ideas about the church and how it should be reformed. During this long friendship they were in constant communication by letters, personal visits, and through their periodicals. They read and discussed together each other's books and editorials. In the Mahoning Baptist Association and in the formative years of the Disciples movement, they were co-workers and recognized leaders. Although they did not always agree, there was an underlying bond of respect and affection that sustained their friendship during this forty year period.

There was a striking similarity in the philosophical and theological heritages of Campbell and Scott. Both had read and been influenced by two of the leading philosophers of the English Enlightenment, Bacon and Locke. They were well-read in the works of the Scottish Independents, particularly Glas, Sandeman, and the Haldanes. Their respective approaches to the interpretation of Scripture were influenced significantly by some of the leading proponents of the grammatico-historical method in the eighteenth and nineteenth century. To a large extent, the philosophical and theological backgrounds they shared resulted in their having common ground. Even before they met, their approaches to theological issues were similar. Each of them had broken with the Presbyterian Church and had repudiated its Calvinistic mode of conversion. They realized that the church was in a desolate condition of fragmentation and sectarian rivalry and needed to be reformed. In their reasoned approaches to the Christian faith, they were endeavoring to restore Primitive Christianity. They accepted the New Testament as sole authority and rejected creeds as tests of orthodoxy. One of the theological issues that was of central importance to each of them was baptism, and on this question their views accorded. Both Scott and Campbell repudiated infant baptism and stressed baptism by immersion of believers for the remission of sins.[49]

Because of the similarities of their backgrounds and theological views and their close personal friendship, Campbell and Scott mutually influenced each other, and each complemented the work of the other. Behind the thought of Scott was the towering intellect of Alexander Campbell. In like manner, Campbell was influenced by the keen, analytical mind and theological acumen of Scott.

In the Reformation of the nineteenth century, Scott viewed himself and the Campbells as co-laborers; each had a distinctive contribution to make.[50] According to Scott, a bold step was taken by Thomas Campbell, who had made a plea for Christian union on the basis of the Bible in his *Declaration and Address*.[51] Following in his father's footsteps, Alexander Campbell in *The Christian Baptist* had disclosed the Ancient Order of the primitive church in the New Testament. Finally, Scott himself took credit for restoring the Ancient Gospel to the church in 1827.

Thomas Campbell's *Declaration and Address*,[52] written in 1809, was a manifesto on Christian union. His main purpose was to stress the universality and essential unity of the church and to show how sectarian rivalries had fragmented the church. The way to effect union was to return to Primitive Christianity as set forth in the New Testament. Thomas Campbell stated that the sole authority for the church and its faith and order is the Scriptures, all creedal formulations being fallacious.

Prior to his meeting with the Campbells, Scott's interests had centered principally around restoring Primitive Christianity. He had given very little consideration to the idea or possibility of Christian union. Campbell's *Declaration and Address* added a new and vital dimension to Scott's thinking. Throughout his life, one of his passionate concerns was to expose the evils of sectarianism and bring about Christian union. This idea found expression in his major theological writings, and especially in his *To Themelion*. The basis of union, according to Scott, is the truth that Jesus Christ is the Messiah and Son of God.

What was implicit in the *Declaration and Address* was made explicit and particularized by Alexander Campbell through the pages of *The Christian Baptist*. The younger Campbell attempted to develop a complete system of doctrines, worship, discipline, and government for the church on the basis of the New Testament. A restoration of the Ancient Order of the church was Campbell's intent. The church must be purified by removing all unauthorized practices and corruptions that had accumulated through the centuries. At this period in his life, Campbell believed that whatever practices of the church were not specifically authorized in the New Testament must be discarded. He would abandon all unscriptural organizations, such as Bible and missionary societies, and all ecclesiastical structures that claimed to exercise control over the local congregations. Each church was an independent, autonomous unit and was to be governed by its own elders (bishops) and deacons. As to the ordinances of the church, Campbell advocated only the observance of the Lord's Supper weekly and baptism by immersion of believers.

Scott accepted Campbell's interpretation of the Ancient Order as the correct understanding of the organizational life and practices of the Early Church. Campbell had already effected the Ancient Order in the Brush Run Church and the Wellsburg Church in Virginia. In this regard, Scott viewed Campbell as a true reformer of the church and followed his lead. Throughout his life Scott wrote much about the organization and life of the church, and his views were in essential agreement with those of Campbell. Scott's interests, however, were centered principally on the restoration and preaching of the Ancient Gospel, Jesus Christ as the Son of God and the six steps in the process of salvation. These were recurring themes in his periodicals and major theological writings. For Scott the Ancient Order and the Ancient Gospel, though different in their scope and emphases, belonged together in the total thrust of the reformation movement of which he and the Campbells were leaders.

One of the prominent themes stated by Campbell was the idea of successive covenants and dispensations that had been established by God to govern the ways he would relate to humanity for a determined period of time.[53] The covenant idea found expression in one of his early writings, the "Sermon on the Law,"[54] which he preached on September 1, 1816, at a meeting of the Redstone Baptist Association at Cross Creek, Virginia. Campbell's sermon was widely read, and in it he expressed many of the ideas that are prominent in Scott's theology. Using Romans 8:3, Campbell made a radical differentiation between the system of Old Testament laws and the Christian Church, or the Mosaic and Christian dispensations. Campbell's argument was that the Christian faith was based on a new covenant that was different from the Old Testament covenant with Moses. The Christian Church was a new institution with its distinctive ordinances, and a new dispensation began with Christ and the new covenant he established. The whole law, ceremonial and moral, was abolished with the coming of Christ. According to Campbell, all arguments and analogies drawn from the Old Testament to support any practice or ordinances of the Christian Church are invalid. Infant baptism as a substitute for circumcision cannot be a part of the Christian faith.

Scott used the idea of successive covenants and dispensations in the history of salvation. His conception of the Ancient Gospel, with its steps in the process of salvation, was based on the idea of the new covenant. In order to be saved, one must fulfill certain conditions of the new covenant that was given by God. Scott had read Campbell's "Sermon on the Law," and it undoubtedly exerted an influence on his thinking on the covenants. One must note, however, that both Campbell and Scott were influenced by the covenant theology that was prominent in the Church of England and the Church of Scotland in the eighteenth century. The covenant idea was also used by Locke, and both Campbell and Scott were strongly influenced by him. Hence, Campbell's "Sermon on the Law" paralleled and corroborated certain ideas Scott had received from Locke and his Presbyterian heritage in the Church of Scotland.

Scott and His Heritage

Walter Scott was a man of the Enlightenment and drank deeply of its spirit. He read and was influenced by some of the prominent thinkers of the era, especially Bacon and Locke. He utilized the Enlightenment philosophical and theological framework to express his major concerns; it was the skeleton that supported the flesh of the gospel. The combined influences of the Scottish Independents and some of the leading biblical scholars of the day led him to concentrate on the restoration of Primitive Christianity and the Scriptures as authoritative for the faith of the church. As his thinking was developing, George Forrester and the Campbells were significant influences on him, giving valuable guidance and setting directions his thought would take.

Within the context of an Enlightenment biblical rationalism, Scott formulated his understanding of the message of the Early Church. The Ancient Gospel entailed a proof of the messiahship of Jesus Christ on the basis of scriptural evidences of prophecy fulfilled and miracles and the six steps in the process of salvation. This was at variance with the orthodox Calvinism prevalent in his day. From the perspective of an Enlightenment understanding of the autonomous individual and human progress, Scott employed certain biblical symbols to develop a postmillennial view of history and the destiny of the American nation. Even though Scott was influenced by these persons and movements, he was a thinker in his own right and had a distinctive contribution to make to the new Disciples movement.

FOOTNOTES

1. Baxter, *Life of Elder Walter Scott*, pp. 36-45.
2. Ibid., pp. 36-37.
3. Ibid., p. 38. See also Hayden, *Early History of the Disciples in the Western Reserve*, pp. 62-63.
4. Baxter, *Life of Elder Walter Scott*, p. 43.
5. For a concise survey of these modern restoration movements, see Alfred T. DeGroot, *The Restoration Principle* (St. Louis: Bethany Press, 1960), pp. 112-113.
6. The movements initiated by Glas, Sandeman, and the Haldanes are discussed by Garrison and DeGroot, *The Disciples of Christ: A History*, pp. 46-53; and Lester G. McAllister and William E. Tucker, *Journey in Faith: A History of the Christian Church (Disciples of Christ)* (St. Louis: Bethany Press, 1975), pp. 94-96.
7. John Glas, *The Works of Mr. John Glas*, 2nd. ed., vols. 1-4 (Perth, Scotland: R. Morison and Son, 1782); vol. 5 (1783).
8. Robert Sandeman, *Letters on Theron and Aspasio, Addressed to the Author*, 2nd. ed., With a Preface, and an Appendix, 2 vols. (Edinburgh: Sands, Donaldson, Murry, and Cochran, 1759); and Robert Sandeman, *An Epistolary Correspondence between Samuel Pike and Robert Sandeman. To which is now annexed, Mr. Pike's Address to the Church, Then Assembling in St. Martin's Le Grand, Now in Paul's Alley, London. Intended as a Conclusion to the Correspondence. Together with Mr. Sandeman's Thoughts on Christianity* (Whitehaven, England: B.N. Dunn, 1798).
9. James Hervey, *Theron and Aspasio: or, A Series of Dialogues and Letters, Upon the Most Important and Interesting Subjects*, 2 vols. (London: J.F. Dove, 1825).
10. Baxter, *Life of Elder Walter Scott*, pp. 47-53, has preserved some extracts from this pamphlet by Henry Errett.
11. Ibid., p. 51.
12. James Alexander Haldane, *Memoirs of the Lives of Robert Haldane of Airthrey, and of His Brother, James Alexander Haldane* (New York: Carter and Brothers, 1857).
13. James Alexander Haldane, *A View of the Social Worship and Ordinances Observed by the First Christians, Drawn from the Sacred Scriptures Alone: Being an Attempt to Enforce Their Divine Obligation; And to Represent the Guilt and Evil Consequences of Neglecting Them* (Edinburgh: J. Ritchie, 1805).
14. For a thorough treatment of the philosophy of Francis Bacon, see Frederick Copleston, *A History of Philosophy*, vol. 3: *Late Mediaeval and Renaissance Philosophy*, pt. 2: *The Revival of Platonism to Suarez* (New York: Image Books, 1963): 103-122.

15. Francis Bacon, *The New Organon and Related Writings*, ed., with an Introduction by Fulton H. Anderson (New York: Bobbs-Merrill, 1960).

16. Ibid., p. 14.

17. Ibid., p. 9.

18. One of the most thorough treatments of the Enlightenment and the different trends of thought it contained is Ernst Cassirer, *The Philosophy of the Enlightenment*, trans. Fritz C.A. Koelln and James P. Pettegrove (Princeton: Princeton University Press, 1951).

19. Scott expressed his views on education in the *United States System*, pp. 20-44.

20. For a discussion of the philosophy of John Locke, see Frederick Copleston, *A History of Philosophy*, vol. 5: *Modern Philosophy: The British Philosophers*, pt. 1: *Hobbes to Paley* (New York: Image Books, 1964): 76-152.

21. John Locke, *The Reasonableness of Christianity, as Delivered in the Scriptures* (Boston: T.B. Wait and Company, 1811).

22. John Locke, *An Essay Concerning Human Understanding* (Philadelphia: James Kay, Jun. and Brother, n.d.).

23. Locke, *The Reasonableness of Christianity*, sec. 33, pp. 234-236.

24. Ibid., secs. 1-3, pp. 1-10.

25. Ibid., sec. 28, pp. 170-171.

26. Ibid., sec. 27, p. 181.

27. Ibid., sec. 34, p. 245.

28. Ibid., sec. 9, p. 25.

29. Ibid., sec. 15, pp. 50-53.

30. Scott, *The Gospel Restored*, pp. 56, 258.

31. Scott, *To Themelion*, p. 67.

32. Scott, *The Gospel Restored*, pp. 9-121.

33. Scott, *To Themelion*, p. 4.

34. Scott, *The Messiahship*, pp. 175-253.

35. See Werner Georg Kummel, *The New Testament: The History of the Investigation of Its Problems*, trans. S. McLean Gilmour and Howard C. Kee (New York: Abingdon, 1972), pp. 51-107, for a discussion of the rise of modern biblical criticism in the seventeenth and eighteenth centuries. Kummel has given attention to some of the leading figures of the age: Locke, Michaelis, Ernesti, Griesbach, Semler, Gabler, and Grotius. It was in this climate of Enlightenment thought that one would place those scholars who employed the grammatico-historical method, especially Locke and Ernesti. See also George Holley Gilbert, *Interpretation of the Bible: A Short History* (New York: Macmillan, 1908), pp. 225-259, for an overview of seventeenth and eighteenth century biblical interpretation.

36. Hans W. Frei, *The Eclipse of Biblical Narrative: A Study in Eigh-*

teenth and Nineteenth Century Hermeneutics (New Haven: Yale University Press, 1974), pp. 166-171, 246-248, 251-255, has discussed the central figures who advocated the grammatico-historical method. Frei has pointed out that Ernesti, one of the more prominent scholars who employed this method, limited the scope of biblical interpretation to the use of words, the historical circumstances governing their use, and the author's intention in writing.

37. See John Locke, *A Paraphrase and Notes on the Epistles of St. Paul to the Galatians, First and Second Corinthians, Romans, and Ephesians. To which is prefixed An Essay for the Understanding of St. Paul's Epistles, by Consulting St. Paul Himself* (Cambridge: Brown, Shattuck, and Company, 1832), pp. 5-24; and Alexander Campbell, *The Christian System: In Reference to the Union of Christians, and a Restoration of Primitive Christianity, As Plead in the Current Reformation* (Nashville: Gospel Advocate Company, 1964), pp. 2-6.

38. Scott, *The Messiahship*, p. 7.

39. James McKnight, *A Harmony of the Four Gospels: In which the Natural Order of each is preserved. With a Paraphrase and Notes*, 2nd. ed., corrected and greatly enlarged, 2 vols. (London: printed for William Strahan, Richard Baldwin, William Johnston, Thomas Longman, and Robert Horsfield, 1763).

40. James McKnight, *A New Literal Translation from the Original Greek, of all the Apostolic Epistles. With a Commentary, and Notes, Philological, Critical, Explanatory, and Practical. To which is added, A History of the Life of the Apostle Paul*, 2nd. ed., 6 vols., *To which is prefixed, An Account of the Life of the Author* (London: printed for Longman, Hurst, Rees, and Orme, Paternoster-Row, 1806).

41. George Benson, *A Paraphrase and Notes on the Epistles of St. Paul to Philemon, 1st Thessalonians, 11d Thessalonians, 1st Timothy, Titus, 11d Timothy. Attempted in Imitation of Mr. Locke's Manner. To which are annexed, Critical Dissertations on Several Subjects, for the Better Understanding of St. Paul's Epistles* (London: printed for Richard Ford, at the Angel in the Poultry, over-against the Compter, 1734); and George Benson, *A Paraphrase and Notes on the Seven (commonly called) Catholic Epistles. viz. St. James, 1St . Peter, 11St. Peter, St. Jude, 1, 11, and 111 of St. John. Attempted in Imitation of Mr. Locke's Manner. To which are annexed Several Critical Dissertations* (London: printed and sold by J. Waugh, in Grace church-street, 1749).

42. George Campbell, *The Four Gospels, Translated from the Greek, With Preliminary Dissertations, and Notes Critical and Explanatory*, 4 vols., With the Author's Last Corrections (Boston: W. Wells, and Thomas B. Wait and Co., 1811), 1:132-176.

43. William Newcome, *An English Harmony of the Four Evangelists, Generally Disposed after the Manner of the Greek of William Newcome*

(Philadelphia: Kimber and Conrad, 1809).

44. Sir Norton Knatchbull, *Annotations upon some difficult Texts in all the Books of the New Testament* (Cambridge: 1693).

45. One of the most popular and widely used of his writings was Joseph Lomas Towers, *Illustrations of Prophecy*, 2 vols. (London: 1796).

46. See William Warburton, *The Works of the Right Reverend William Warburton, D.D. Lord Bishop of Gloucester*, new ed., 12 vols., *To which is prefixed a Discourse by Way of General Preface; containing Some Account of the Life, Writings, and Character of the Author*, by Richard Hurd, D.D. Lord Bishop of Worcester (London: printed by Luke Hansard & Sons, near Lincoln's Inn Fields, 1811).

47. One of the works to which Scott may have had access was Sir Isaac Newton, *Observations upon the Prophecies of Daniel, and the Apocalypse of St. John*, 2 pts. (London: printed by J. Darby and T. Brown, and sold by J. Roberts, 1733).

48. Alexander Campbell, *The Sacred Writings of the Apostles and Evangelists of Jesus Christ, Commonly Styled the New Testament, translated from the original Greek by George Campbell, James Macknight, and Philip Doddridge, with prefaces, various emendations, and an appendix by Alexander Campbell*, 3rd ed. (Bethany, Brooke Co., Va.: Alexander Campbell, 1832), p. 56; and *The Millennial Harbinger* 5 (May 1834): 199. One of the most thorough studies of Alexander Campbell's use of the grammatico-historical method is Cecil K. Thomas, *Alexander Campbell and His New Version* (St. Louis: Bethany Press, 1958), pp. 147-169.

49. Alexander Campbell, "Events of 1823 and 1827," *The Millennial Harbinger*, n.s., 2 (October 1838): 468.

50. Scott, *The Gospel Restored*, pp. v-vi.

51. Thomas Campbell, *Declaration and Address*, With an introduction by William Robinson (Birmingham, England: Berean Press, 1951).

52. See Lester G. McAllister, *Thomas Campbell: Man of the Book* (St. Louis: Bethany Press, 1954), pp. 105-137, for a concise analysis and summary of the main ideas expressed in the *Declaration and Address*.

53. Winfred Ernest Garrison, *Alexander Campbell's Theology: Its Sources and Historical Setting* (St. Louis: Christian Publishing Company, 1900), pp. 129-158, has shown the influence of the Dutch theologians, Cocceius and Witsius, on Campbell's ideas of the covenants. He has also indicated the extent to which the covenant theology pervaded the Church of England and the Church of Scotland in the eighteenth century.

54. *The Millennial Harbinger*, ser. 3, 3 (September 1846): 493-521.

CHAPTER THREE

COME NOW, LET US REASON TOGETHER

The Old Testament Scriptures prove their own "divine" authenticity by proving that their author is the Omniscient God.

The New Testament proves its divine authenticity by proving that Jesus Christ is the Messiah, the Son of God.

Walter Scott, *The Messiahship*, p. 33.

Brethren, give me my Bible, my Head, and Brother William Hayden, and we will go out and convert the world.

Words of Walter Scott, quoted in A.S. Hayden, *Early History of the Disciples in the Western Reserve, Ohio*, p. 174.

In the unfolding saga of America, the preachers and especially the revivalists have written a significant chapter. On the Mayflower, Elder William Brewster was pastor of the small Pilgrim band. Increase and Cotton

Mather, the Puritan divines, made an impact on Colonial America through their writings and preaching. During the Great Awakening of the early and mid-eighteenth century Jonathan Edwards and George Whitefield preached with eloquence. Their efforts brought a new surge of piety to Colonial America prior to the Revolutionary War. In the latter eighteenth and early nineteenth century the Second Great Awakening began on the eastern seaboard and surged westward. As it reached into the frontier regions it was called by many the Great Western Revival.

During these formative years of the new nation, as people went westward in search of a new life and braved the dangers of frontier living, the church was close behind them. These frontier folks all needed saving faith, so the church reasoned. Rising to meet the need of the hour were the preachers of the Word, those nameless advocates of the gospel. Going out and searching for the lost souls, they preached the good news and sought to convert them to the way of Christ. In so doing it was their hope to create a Christian nation, and beyond that to convert the world to the cause of the Kingdom of God.

There were the travelling preachers, the revivalists, and the circuit riders. Methodists, Baptists, Presbyterians, Christians, and Disciples all vied for their souls and their commitments. They came to the rolling hills of Tennessee, throughout Kentucky, the Ohio valley, and northeastern Ohio. Special revivals broke out almost spontaneously in Logan County and Cane Ridge, Kentucky. Countless souls heard the gospel proclaimed in the power of the Spirit. The preachers could be found in revivals or camp meetings, under a clump of trees or in an open space, in a home or log church newly built. Wherever men and women were hungry for the saving Word, there were the preachers to feed them the solid food of the gospel.

These frontier preachers were a brave and dauntless group, ready to go any place at any time where the sinful were in need of salvation. There was about them a spirit of self-abandonment. No place was too remote or out of the way, no settlement too small for them to visit and preach. Going on foot or horseback, along rough trails cut through the wilderness, these proclaimers of the good tidings received little if any pay — a few dollars or whatever collection could be taken up from the assembled multitudes. Come rain or sleet, blizzards or cloudbursts, sunny or dreary days, they still journeyed from settlement to settlement and church to church. Along the way they might encounter bears, wildcats, wolves, or perhaps an unfriendly band of Indians looking for another white man's scalp. Still, they travelled and they preached! These apostles of the Lord crossed swollen streams and went over snow covered mountains in search of souls that needed the saving Word.

At night these journeymen slept in a cabin on a dirt floor by the fire or in a barn with hay for a bed and pillow. If they were fortunate one of the good brothers or sisters let them sleep in one of their beds. For food they ate whatever the local hospitality could offer — a piece of beef or pork and some cornbread, maybe a chicken dinner. These bold but humble spirits were grateful for whatever the Lord provided. Cold and wet, weary and saddle sore from riding their mare, some had to preach in a suit they had slept in the night before. Sometimes, if the occasion called for it, they preached three times a day and baptized their converts in ice cold water from a nearby creek or river. Many died young from long exposure to the elements; few lived to enjoy an old age.

Besides a few belongings, they took with them their Bibles and their heartfelt desire that others would hear the good news of salvation and accept it. Whatever doctrinal differences might exist between their denominations, they were all in agreement that the Bible was the divinely revealed Word inspired by the Holy Spirit and that Jesus Christ was Saviour of the world. Their one aim was to make the gospel message strike the hearts of men and women, convict them of their sins, and lead them to the Lord Jesus Christ.

Standing tall in this grand heritage of frontier revival preachers was Walter Scott. He, like the others, preached Jesus Christ and he preached from the Bible. But what did he believe about Jesus Christ and the Bible? How did he think? What did he believe about the gospel? To these issues we now turn.

The Man, His Mind and Pen

Walter Scott was an evangelist, editor, teacher, and writer; the focus of his theological writings was the Christian faith as understood on the basis of the Old and New Testaments. In many instances, he quoted long passages of Scripture or cited a number of different texts to substantiate a point. Numerous seventeenth and eighteenth century biblical scholars and commentators were utilized by him in his writings.[1] Scott possessed a sense of history, displaying a broad knowledge of the history of the church and theology; however, his interest centered mainly in the Enlightenment era and the thinking of Bacon and Locke.

The style of Scott's writing is argumentative and polemic, especially against Calvinism and Catholicism. Also, he opposed the sectarianism of his day and extreme emotionalism in religion. For Scott, as with Locke, religious truths were basically propositional in nature; they were reasonable and substantiated on the basis of evidences in Scripture. The gospel in its fundamental sense consisted of a basic proposition revealed in Scripture, namely, that Jesus Christ is the Son of God and Messiah. One believed this truth on the basis of proofs and evidences that were convincing to human reason. This argumentative approach to the Christian faith gave to much of Scott's writings an objective, legalistic quality.

In his writings about the Christian faith Scott used the methods of analysis, synthesis, and induction. A pronounced quality of his writings was a breaking down and analyzing of the whole of the faith into smaller segments, divisions, and steps. For example, Christianity was analyzed in terms of three divisions: the evangelical, transitional, and ecclesiastical; the process of salvation entailed six steps in sequence. Scott also analyzed the Scriptures in terms of types and antitypes, symbols, and prophecies. By viewing these types and antitypes and prophecies fulfilled with the coming of Christ, his synthesizing led him to conclude that the Scriptures were a harmonious whole and inspired by the Holy Spirit. In line with the thinking of Enlightenment rationalism, Scott applied Bacon's method of induction to the Scriptures, examining a number of particular texts and arriving at a general principle. Having established a propositional truth or principle, he made this the basis from which other truths or components of the faith could be understand. Induction can be seen in Scott's approach to the Person of Jesus Christ. The truth that Jesus Christ is the Messiah and Son of God was arrived at by an inductive examination of the Scriptures, in particular, miracles and the fulfillment of prophecies. The messiahship of Jesus Christ, then, was the basis for understanding other truths concerning the meaning of salvation, the church, and Christian union.

Scott was a churchman who wrote for the church as he understood it. He was very much concerned for the life of the church, its members, and persons making a decision for the Christian faith. As an evangelist and editor, Scott understood himself as preaching and writing to make the Ancient Gospel reasonable to ministers and laypersons in the church. This concern to make the Christian faith intelligible pulsated throughout the pages of his theological works and periodicals. Equally significant was his passionate concern to have the church of his day overcome sectarian rivalries and restore its unity.

The Truths of God: Natural and Revealed

For Scott, valid religious knowledge could be derived

from both human reason and the revelation contained in the Scriptures, and on this issue he was strongly influenced by John Locke and Henry Lord Brougham. Locke's *An Essay Concerning Human Understanding* and *The Reasonableness of Christianity* were determinative to a large extent for Scott's theory of knowledge and the overall structure of his thought. Following Locke, Scott believed that certain truths about God could be understood by human reason alone. The truths of faith revealed in the Scriptures, however, were beyond reason but were not contrary to or inconsistent with reason.[2]

In order to elaborate further on the relationship of reason and revelation, Scott referred to Henry Lord Brougham's *A Discourse of Natural Theology.*[3] Scott quoted from Brougham, gave a summary of his views on natural and revealed theology, and affirmed his agreement with Brougham's position.[4] Brougham endeavored to show that there is validity in natural theology, which is able to demonstrate the existence of one living God and the attributes of power, wisdom, and goodness. The Apostle Paul stated it clearly: "Ever since the creation of the world his invisible nature, namely, his eternal power and deity, has been clearly perceived in the things that have been made" (Rom. 1:20). In addition to these truths, natural theology gives a reasoned base and strength to revealed theology, because all the arguments supporting revelation presuppose those truths established by natural theology. The truths of revelation and the evidences attesting to them would be greatly weakened if the support given them by natural theology were removed. Further, if the claims of natural theology are false, revelation cannot be true. According to Brougham, both natural theology and revealed theology rest on evidences that are reasonable. Hence, God is known in His works and His word on the basis of evidences. As natural theology demonstrates God's existence and power, so the revelation in Scripture declares the will of God, His purpose of bringing life and immortality to humankind, and the way He should be worshipped.[5]

Brougham's distinction between natural and revealed theology was appropriated by Scott. According to him, the law of Moses is in its essential features a restatement of the basic propositions of natural theology concerning the one living God and His creativity.[6] As there is harmony in the Scriptures, so harmony is present in nature, where intelligent design and unity of purpose can be discerned. Scott agreed with the psalmist that the natural world clearly reveals God: "The heavens are telling the glory of God; and the firmament proclaims his handiwork" (Psa. 19:1). Scott also stated his understanding of natural and revealed theology, the truths of which rest upon reasonable evidences, in terms of the "general proposition" and the "particular proposition." On these two propositions and the relationship that should exist between them, Scott wrote:

> The proposition of the Deists that there is one living and true God, we name the general proposition, because it is believed by all men, Jews, Gentiles, and the church of God; and with the author of the Discourse of Natural Theology, we admit its credibility, even on scientific principles. The Christian proposition, that Jesus is God's Son, we style the particular one, because it is believed only by a portion of mankind, who depend for their

belief of it on a special proof, differing in many points from the universal evidence, which the works of nature every where supply of the divine existence and character. The first of these propositions is received by Deists, and both of them by Christians. The former is proved by the works of nature; the latter by the words of revelation. And as Revelation does not say the first is false, so nature does not assert the last to be impossible. For if nature show that there is a God, Revelation may show that there is also a Son of God, experience demonstrating that where there is one being there may be another of a like nature.[7]

The Scriptures: Oracles of the Holy Spirit

Although Scott affirmed the tenets of natural theology and their necessity, his main concerns were the truths revealed by God in the Scriptures. For Scott, Christianity was a revealed religion, and all the truths regarding the salvation of humankind were to be found in the Scriptures. The Old and New Testaments contained the revelation from God that was imparted verbally to the prophets and apostles by the Holy Spirit.[8]

In Scott's thinking there was a close relationship between the Scriptures, the Holy Spirit, and Jesus Christ, such that one cannot be understood without the others. According to him, the central theme of the Scriptures and the key to their interpretation was the messiahship of Jesus Christ. The Old and New Testaments, containing the testimony of the prophets and apostles, proved that Jesus Christ is the Messiah and Son of God on the basis of the evidences of miracles and prophecy fulfilled. The Scriptures in showing this internal congruity proved, according to Scott, that they were inspired by the Holy Spirit.[9] On the basis of internal evidences, then, the Scriptures demonstrated their authority and authenticity; "so it, the word of God, contains within itself proof positive of its own heavenly inspiration."[10] Since the Old and New Testaments together witnessed to the truth that Jesus Christ is the Messiah, Scott conceived the Scriptures to be a perfectly harmonious whole. In his own words:

> It is so with the Bible and New Testament; the internal congruity of their several parts, the admirable agreement of the facts of the one, with the prophecies of the other, the felicity with which the oracle gradually develops itself . . . all demonstrate that the author of nature is the author of revelation.[11]

Another of the central features of Scott's thinking on the Scriptures and the Christian faith was his doctrine of the Holy Spirit, which he formulated in *The Gospel Restored* and especially in his treatise, *A Discourse on the Holy Spirit*. In this latter work, Scott developed his ideas in terms of the three divine missions: the mission of Jesus Christ to the Jews, the mission of the apostles to the world, and the mission of the Holy Spirit to the church.[12] In his discussion of the Holy Spirit and the three divine missions, one can see clearly Scott's penchant for careful analysis and categorization. The missions, each separate and distinct, were defined in terms of persons, terminations, and designs. To make these as clear as possible, he stated the three missions in propositional form:

> Proposition 1: Jesus Christ was personally a missionary only to the Jews; his mission terminated on that people;

and the designs of it were to proclaim the gospel, and to teach those among men who believed it.

Proposition 2: The Apostles were missionaries to the whole world; their mission terminated on mankind and its design was to proclaim the gospel, and to teach those among men who believed it.

Proposition 3: The Holy Spirit was a missionary to the church. His mission terminated on that institution, and the designs of it were to comfort the disciples, glorify Jesus Christ as the true Messiah, and to convince the world of sin, righteousness, and judgment.[13]

Scott advanced a theory of verbal inspiration of Scripture that was solidly founded on his inductive investigation of its claims. The Holy Spirit spoke to the prophets and apostles, imparting to them truths, propositions, and convincing evidences for the messiahship of Jesus Christ.[14] In terms of the Christian faith, the Holy Spirit worked only through the church, the body of Christ, whose members were filled with the Holy Spirit. The apostles wrote only as the Spirit directed them in producing the New Testament.

According to Scott's understanding, the Holy Spirit spoke through the preaching of the apostles in terms of the convincing evidences for faith. He pointed out that the apostles preached, whereas it was the role of the Spirit to convince; hence, the mission of the apostles was different from that of the Holy Spirit.[15] Scott was saying that preaching in his day as well as in the apostolic age was verbalizing and explaining what was written in the Scriptures, and the evidences in Scripture supporting faith were verbally inspired by the Holy Spirit. The Word (Scriptures) and the Spirit belonged together in this sense, and the Spirit did the convincing for the truth of the messiahship of Jesus Christ through the medium of the apostolic preaching.[16] It was true, as Paul wrote, "No one can say 'Jesus is Lord' except by the Holy Spirit" (I Cor. 12:3).

In *A Discourse on the Holy Spirit*, one of Scott's primary purposes was to present an alternative to the Calvinistic mode of conversion; hence, there is a decidedly polemical cast to his writing. According to the prevailing Calvinism on the American frontier in the early nineteenth century, humankind was totally depraved through original sin and was incapable of taking the first step towards salvation. A direct action of the Holy Spirit on the soul of the person was required in order to effect regeneration. As a result of the Spirit's mysterious action, called "regenerating grace" or "enabling grace," one had the saving experience and was able to exercise faith and repentance. Over against the Calvinistic scheme of conversion, Scott presented a rational view of the Holy Spirit's role in the inspiration of the Scriptures and in the conversion of the individual. His main endeavor was to show that the Holy Spirit exercised a convincing role on the mind through the evidences in the Scriptures and the apostolic preaching. The individual can hear the Word and respond in faith to the reasoning and convincing of the Holy Spirit. According to Scott's rational view of the Scriptures and conversion, the Holy Spirit does not act directly on the believer's soul to regenerate him; prior to faith the Spirit is external.

If the Holy Spirit does not enter the soul of the sinner, how can he "convince" him? I answer that God convinces us as we convince one another — by truth and argument. Can the Holy Spirit do nothing for a person unless he enters that person? Did he glorify Christ by entering him, or by enlightening the Apostles on his character? As, then, the Spirit glorified Christ without entering him, so he can convince sinners without entering and dwelling in them. Let preachers, and all who believe, hold forth the word of the Spirit to the people: let them forbear calling it a "dead letter," and the Spirit shall soon convince sinners of sin. . . . Is it nowhere said in Scripture, that the Spirit must convince us of sin? Yes; but we have already seen how he does this: namely, by the word of God, preached — not by going into the souls of sinners.[17]

The Holy Spirit enters as a gift to the believer subsequent to baptism for the remission of sins (Acts 2:38). One of the underlying presuppositions operative in Scott's conception of conversion was the optimistic Enlightenment view of the autonomous individual who had the ability to weigh the evidences and make an intelligent response in faith for the Christian gospel.

A Person is the Creed

From reading and studying the Scriptures, Scott formulated his fundamental conviction that the basis of Christianity is the belief that Jesus Christ is the Messiah and Son of God. For Scott's biblical rationalism, this was the Creed of Christianity or, as he often referred to it, "the Golden Oracle." A chain of influences in his own personal life and from his study guided him to this conception, which was the pivotal point for the whole of his theology. Three persons were especially significant in this regard. First, George Forrester pointed Scott to the Scriptures as the central authority for the Christian faith and to the necessity of returning to the fundamentals of Primitive Christianity. Scott's relationship with Forrester intensified his interest in studying the Scriptures for himself, discerning their central truths, and engaging in continuing theological study. The second person was John Locke, who emphasized that Christianity is based on the proposition that Jesus Christ is the Messiah. This proposition was established on the basis of evidences of miracles and prophecy fulfilled. Faith and repentance were necessary for one to enter the new covenant. Third, the impact of Henry Errett, the Scotch Baptist, was significant. Scott received from Errett, through his lectures on the four Gospels and in personal conversation, a clear understanding that the messiahship of Jesus Christ was central for Christianity.

In Scott's thinking, the biblical truth that Jesus Christ is the Messiah and Son of God was first revealed to humankind by God. It was declared audibly at the baptism of Jesus and was in fact the only direct communication made by God the Father to the world;[18] it was a "divine oracle."[19]

For Scott, Christianity entails a fundamental proposition, but it is a proposition about a person, Jesus Christ. Thus, in all that Scott wrote about Jesus Christ as the Messiah there was a twofold emphasis — the rational and the personal. Christianity is a rational faith because it is based upon a proposition about Jesus Christ and supported by evidences of miracles and the fulfillment of prophecy. According to Scott's understanding of the Scriptures, Christianity is a proof and a logic. One is to understand the messiahship of Jesus Christ "as the problematic element of the gospel, that is the proposition which rests on proof."[20] Religious truth, then, was revealed to humanity by God in terms of rational propositions that could be stated in human language. Regarding this rational aspect of the Christian faith, he noted:

> Again; the faith of the Gospel is not a truth without a proof — something spoken with nothing to prove it true. The Christian faith, like all other faith, belongs to the science of inference — reason — logic, and depends for its reception in society on proof.[21]

Scott's understanding of Jesus Christ and faith was also expressed in strongly personal terms. The Christian faith is not only rational assent to a proposition, but it is also a trusting relationship and commitment to Jesus Christ. In his own words:

> Now Christ is made unto us the medium of all this knowledge and consolation; and his ministrations, therefore, as well as his exalted and divine nature and excellence, presents him to us as the personage most worthy of our confidence, reverence, and affection. Those best acquainted with him have always loved him most. . . . My attachment for him is not a blind attachment; but one that grows out of a long and patient inquiry into the Christian Religion, and serious meditation upon what they say, of the human family and of Him in particular, the Redeemer of that family.[22]

Scott's preaching centered principally on Jesus Christ and the steps in the process of salvation. The chief concern of any preacher is to point sinners to Jesus Christ, the person, so that through Him they might receive salvation. For Scott, the essence of the Christian faith is not assenting to a series of doctrinal statements or subscribing to a creedal formulation but having a personal relationship with Jesus Christ and obeying His teachings. J.J. Haley has expressed this personal element by stating that for Scott, "Faith was personal conviction concerning a personal Saviour, the outcome of which was personal salvation and personal character."[23]

Miracles Performed and Prophecies Fulfilled

Jesus Christ is the Messiah and Son of God! In Scott's thinking, this was the principal doctrine preached throughout the Early Church, and it must be preached in the present. This proposition, which was the cornerstone of his whole theology, was proved on the basis of the scriptural evidences of miracles and prophecies fulfilled.

In the New Testament, according to Scott, there are various classifications of miracles in terms of who performed them and on whom they were performed. The apostles themselves, having received the gift of the Holy Spirit, were able to work miracles.[24] In the book of Revelation John is entrusted with the miracle of a revelation of Christ in His glory.[25] For Scott the most important miracles were those by Christ Himself and those wrought on Him, both classes giving evidences for the messiahship on the basis of observation and experience (Locke). Regarding these miracles and what they entailed Scott wrote:

> My use of the term is this. Those who saw miracles performed on the persons of others had the evidence of observation; and those who felt them performed on

> their own persons had the evidence of experience for the Messiahship. . . . Experience and observation were, therefore, 'the' tests, 'the' original tests of the Christian miracles.[26]

In Scott's preaching and writing the principal evidences supporting the messiahship were the miracles performed on Jesus Christ Himself.[27] In the Old and New Testaments miracles were of two kinds — power and foreknowledge. A miracle of power would be the resurrection of a dead man, whereas to foretell that resurrection would be a miracle of foreknowledge. Thus, all the prophecies recorded in the Old Testament regarding the miracles that would be wrought on the Messiah were miracles of foreknowledge. When any miracle was performed, either of power or foreknowledge (prophecy), God was present and acting in a supernatural manner. Scott conceived the miracles wrought on Christ Himself, those of power and foreknowledge, to be composite or a "sui generis" series of miracles,[28] and they constituted the greatest proof for the messiahship. In his writings he focused on seven miracles or events in the life of Christ and briefly described each of these:

1. The Incarnation — a miraculous manifestation of God in the flesh.

2. The Installation — a miraculous recognition of the Messiah.

3. The Transfiguration — a miraculous rehearsal of eternal life.

4. His Death — a miraculous redemption of the race.

5. His Resurrection — a miracle of light.

6. His Ascension — a miracle of hope.

7. His Glorification — a miracle of man on God's throne.[29]

The procedure Scott used was to state the miracle, quote the Old Testament prophecies and types prefiguring it, and show how they were fulfilled in the life of Christ. Most of the Old Testament prophecies were derived from the Psalms, Isaiah, and Daniel.[30] One of the central features in his treatment of the miracles was to point out what it meant concerning the messiahship. The New Testament reports from the Gospels, Acts, and the Epistles were cited as evidence, along with quotes and references from the various biblical scholars at his disposal.

The Incarnation, Inauguration, and Transfiguration

The first miracle was the incarnation,[31] the coming of God in the flesh. It was the basis for the other six miracles performed on Christ, thereby offering proof for the messiahship. For Scott, it was important that the incarnation occurred, but he did not treat the nature of the union of God and humanity in the Person of Jesus Christ, such as was characteristic of the speculative thinking in the Early Church.

The incarnation was "the greatest truth in history,"[32] for which there was no equal. It was uniquely "the mystery" (I Cor. 15:51; Rev. 1:20), as he explained at some length:

In our religion there are many mysteries, or opened secrets — many things, which, till revealed in Christianity, were unknown to the world. But though these are numerous, only one of them is marked out definitely as "the mystery" — only one of them is styled, by way of eminence, "to mysterion" the mystery. . . . And it is thus named because before the era of Christ it was unknown both to Jews and Gentiles. . . . Our reconciliation to God and to one another by the blood of Christ, our sanctification by the Spirit, our organization under Christ, our resurrection, the last judgment, the burning of the world, and eternal life are all mysteries, but none of them is styled the great mystery. . . . there is a secret which from the foundation of the world was hid in God, dropped into prophecy, afterward made good in history, and finally offered for faith to all nations, which in sublimity and glory excels all these as far as the splendors of the meridian sun excel the twinklings of the most distant of the fixed stars. Paul styles it not only the great but the "incontrovertibly great" mystery or revelation. Is it asked then what this is? "God was manifest in the flesh!"[33]

As the great mystery, the incarnation was the central truth of the Christian faith.[34] The incarnation, the truth that God was manifested in the flesh, was for the purpose of Christ's sacrificial death. It was the miracle of the incarnation that made possible the redemption of humankind from sin and offered the basis for eternal life.[35]

The baptism of Jesus, when He was publicly declared by God to be His Son, was the occasion of His inauguration (installation) into the messianic office and constituted the second of the miracles.[36] Jesus Christ was, therefore, the Redeemer of the world by the direct authority of God Himself and was engaged in a divine mission.[37] Just as the baptism opened His ministry with the descent of the Holy Spirit, so His mission closed at

Pentecost when the Spirit descended on the assembled multitude.[38]

Scott pointed to the transfiguration[39] as a manifestation of the future glory of Jesus Christ when His kingdom would come with power. It was a glorious miracle granted to three of the disciples, and like the other miracles was intended to convince others that Jesus Christ is the Messiah. Concerning this miracle Scott wrote:

> The transfiguration is, therefore, a glimpse, vouchsafed three of the twelve, of the glory to be revealed at the Lord's second coming. It is a daguerrotype, or rather a "tableau vivant," of the resurrection state in which Christ appears as king, and Moses and Elias, the representatives of his people, of whom some will be raised from the dead like Moses, and some transfigured like Elias. What points soever are found in the tableau of the transfiguration, the same will form elements of the kingdom of glory at its inauguration by God the Father.[40]

The Death of Christ

In Scott's understanding of Jesus Christ and the miracles wrought on him, one of the focal points was His death.[41] Scott referred to the death of Christ as "the mother of miracles"; so significant was this event that "it works such marvels on earth that it may of itself alone be said to prove the Messiahship of our Lord."[42] In his discussion of the death of Christ and the atonement, one notes the polemical cast to his argument that was directed against the orthodox Calvinistic idea of the limited atonement for the elect alone.[43] He expressed his understanding of the meaning of Christ's death by stating and defending three propositions:

1. Adam sinned for all.
2. Christ died for all.
3. Christ is preached to all.[44]

The death of Christ, which was voluntary and violent, was prophesied in Daniel 9, Psalm 40, and Isaiah 53.[45] The fulfillment of these prophecies in the life and death of Christ proved his messiahship. His sacrificial death was an example of obedience to God, whereby He gave His life voluntarily so that He might rise again and redeem humankind.[46] The death and resurrection of Christ were closely related and belonged together in Scott's view of the redeeming work of God. Though he discussed the death and resurrection as separate miracles, all that he wrote concerning the meaning of Christ's atoning death was in light of the resurrection.

Scott's thinking on the death of Christ revolved around two basic themes. First, the sin of humanity necessitated Christ's coming and His sacrificial death to destroy the powers of death, sin, and Satan. Second, he formulated a penal substitutionary theory of atonement by the blood of Christ.

Because of the sin and disobedience of humanity to the Creator, the atoning death of Christ was a necessity. Christ was the bearer of the sins of all humankind, and to his death Scott applied the ideas of penal substitution and sacrifice. Being very specific on these he wrote:

> It was necessary, therefore, before man could re-ascend, that the Creator should provide a redeemer, who should be not only Adam's antithesis but his own also — himself and another at the same time! This he did in his own Son; who to meet our case was manifested in flesh, and became "substitutionally" animal, guilty, condemned,

weak, mortal; but at the same time "personally" spiritual, holy, just, powerful, and immortal.[47]

In discussing the meaning of the atoning death, Scott juxtaposed Adam and Christ (I Cor. 15:21-22), comparing their persons, acts, and the effects of their actions. As Adam was the generic head of the race, Christ was the regenerative head. Adam's disobedience brought death and the loss of immortality to humanity, whereas Christ's death and resurrection brought the destruction of death and immortality to all who believed. Adam and Christ, besides being historical persons, were also potentialities and powers.[48] Scott expressed this relationship between Adam and Christ on sin and the atonement most succinctly by again stating two propositions.

1. God has laid the sin of Adam on all men.
2. And the sins of all men on Christ.[49]

In His death and resurrection Christ destroyed the power of death and bondage to sin and Satan. Humanity was thereby delivered from its bondage to these powers and offered life and immortality. Scott explained this by writing:

> It is not then as a "redeemer" but an "avenger" the Messiah is first promised. His first work is not to save, but destroy — "destroy death and him that had the power of death, that is the devil." His second is "to deliver those, who through fear of death, were all their lifetime subject to bondage." The second part is reached only through the first, that is by the destruction of the works of the devil the Lord reaches our salvation.[50]

The death of Christ was viewed by Scott also as a ransom given for the redemption of humanity from sin.

COME NOW, LET US REASON TOGETHER

In his atoning death by substitution, Christ gave his life
as a "ransom for many," to die in our stead (Gal. 3:13).[51]
By the "many," Scott meant that Christ died "instead of
Adam and in him all men."[52] He further stated what
atonement by substitution meant.

> As for the suffering of Christ, it is perhaps unnecessary
> to quote any thing to show for what he died. "Anti" is
> the proper Greek word for "instead of," and is used in
> the New Testament in regard to his death. "The Son of
> Man came not to be ministered, but to minister, and to
> give his life a ransom 'anti polon,' instead of
> many." . . . Christ, therefore, is our great substitution in
> Law, the antitype of all the blood that was spilt from the
> fall to the time of his death.[53]

An integral aspect of Scott's theology was a penal
substitutionary theory of the atonement by the blood of
Christ, which showed the justice and mercy of God.[54]
Christ was the "sacrificial victim,"[55] and our redemption
was through this act of "substitution, or salvation by
blood poured from the veins of a person in the house of
David."[56] By this, Scott did not mean that the material
aspects of the blood Christ shed was atoning. It was
Christ's life or soul carried in His blood (life-blood) that
was the means of atonement. Basing his argument on
Lev. 17:11 and applying it to the blood of Christ, Scott
explained:

> God has appointed it as the means of atonement for
> your sins. But it is the means of atonement as the bearer
> of the soul. It is not, therefore, the matter of the blood
> that atones, but the "soul or life that resides in it;" so
> that the soul (or life in the blood) of the offered victim,
> atones for the soul (or life) of the man who offers
> it. . . . the life of a beast was a very inadequate substitute

for the life of a man. It was therefore only for the time being. It was provisional till Christ, in whose blood a life was carried that was altogether precious, pure, and holy. This life-blood alone atoned, expiated, and propitiated.[57]

By the death of Christ as a substitution by His blood, humankind was reconciled to the Father. The conscience of the worshipper was purged, cleansed, and perfected by His blood; the guilt of sin and fear of punishment were thereby removed through baptism. For Scott, redemption was twofold, involving both the intellect and the conscience. Belief in Jesus Christ as the Messiah, as evidenced by miracles and prophecy, purified the understanding, but the remission of sins by the blood of Christ was effected in baptism.[58]

The Resurrection, Ascension, and Glorification

The resurrection of Jesus Christ, according to Scott, was "the greatest fact in history."[59] It was foreseen by God, prophesied in the Old Testament,[60] and brought about by His power. As an historical fact, the resurrection of Christ was another of the great miracles wrought on Him and thereby proved His messiahship.[61] In his treatment of this miracle, Scott was concerned principally with the meaning and effects of the resurrection according to the testimony of the Scriptures, not with the nature of the resurrected body of Christ.

The key to the whole redemptive work of God was the resurrection of Christ, although it was inseparable from His death. Concerning the death and resurrection, Scott's view was that as sin and death came through

Adam, righteousness and immortality were brought about by Christ. The death and resurrection of Christ were the only miraculous events capable of destroying the powers of sin and death.[62] Even though the death and resurrection of Christ belonged together, the crucial event and key to the redemptive act of Christ was the resurrection. Regarding the centrality and significance of the resurrection, Scott sated:

> In the work of Adam and the work of Christ we have the genesis and regenesis — the generative and regenerative elements of the revealed system. And the key to the truth and authority of the whole is the resurrection of the Messiah. This being proved true, all is proved true. It is the pivot on which all turns.[63]

The ascension[64] and glorification[65] were the two concluding miracles performed on Christ. Both of these miracles were closely related in that they pertained to the resurrected and exalted state of Christ, and the ascension was the means by which Christ entered His status of glory. Scott's main concern in the ascension was to show that there were various Old Testament types and ascensions prefiguring the ascension of Christ,[66] and these prophecies and the miracle itself provided scriptural evidences to prove His messiahship.[67]

The glorification of Christ, like the ascension, was prophesied in the Old Testament.[68] The difference between many of the Old Testament figures and Christ was that they were translated to heaven, but only Christ was glorified. In His ascension to heaven, Christ was seated at the right hand of God, a position of exaltation, power, and honor. With this final miracle of glorification performed on Christ, all the messianic prophecies were

111

fulfilled, thus confirming the truth of His messiahship.[69]
Jesus Himself had made this clear, following His resurrection, when He told the disciples: "These are my
words which I spoke to you, while I was still with you,
that everything written about me in the law of Moses
and the prophets and the psalms must be fulfilled"
(Luke 24:44).

On This Rock I Will Build My Church

In Scott's preaching and theological writing, the messiahship of Jesus Christ is central. Scott's theology is
essentially a rational and biblically centered interpretation of the Person of Jesus Christ. All that he wrote
about salvation, the church, and Christian union was
based upon and derived from this conception concerning the messiahship of Jesus Christ. In his understanding of the founding of the church, which he equated
with the kingdom of God, the main events were the
baptism of Jesus and the confession of Simon Peter at
Caesarea Philippi: "You are the Christ, the Son of the
living God" (Matt. 16:16). On both of these occasions,
the messiahship of Jesus Christ was crucial; hence, the
church was founded on this belief. At Caesarea Philippi,
the keys of the kingdom were given to Peter, and in his
thinking the keys were faith, repentance, baptism for
the remission of sins, and the gift of the Holy Spirit.[70]
The keys of the kingdom (church) were therefore identical with the keys to salvation, both being based upon
the messiahship of Jesus Christ.

In addition to being the cornerstone of the church

and salvation, belief in Jesus Christ as Messiah and Son of God was the fundamental principle upon which Christian union could be effected.[71] Christian union was one of the central themes for Scott, Campbell, and the other Reformers. In his understanding of the Christian faith, Scott believed that it was necessary to restore the Ancient Gospel; Campbell had already recovered the Ancient Order. The Ancient Gospel, the messiahship of Jesus Christ and the steps in the process of salvation, was the message to be preached to all persons so that they might be converted and enter the church. It was also the basis upon which all Christians could be united in the church. Further, the union of all the churches was a necessary prelude to the coming millennial age.

Belief in the messiahship of Jesus Christ figured prominently in Scott's attempt to form an overall understanding of the Christian faith. He organized Christianity and its tenets in various ways, prominent among which was the tripartite division into the messiahship, doctrine, and proof.[72] The basic idea underlying his attempt to organize the Christian faith under these categories concerned his understanding of Jesus and his teachings. According to Scott, the only proposition in the Scriptures that needs to be proved is that Jesus Christ is the Messiah and Son of God. This can be established on the basis of the miracles and the fulfillment of prophecy. Having proved the messiahship of Jesus, it was Scott's contention that nothing He taught (doctrine) could be false. Christ's teachings are true and authoritative because He is the Messiah and cannot err.[73] The four Gospel writers reported accurately Jesus' teachings, and the four Gospels harmonized insofar as these teachings are concerned.

The Christian faith could also be generalized in regard to the persons to whom the preaching and teachings were directed. In this respect, Scott organized Christianity into three divisions — the evangelical, transitional, and ecclesiastical.[74] The evangelical division entailed the preaching of the Ancient Gospel to the world. It involved a presentation of the proposition that Jesus Christ is the Messiah, the scriptural evidences supporting it, and the steps in the process of salvation. The transitional division concerned baptism, whereby the believer was transferred from the world to the church. The transitional also connected the evangelical and the third or ecclesiastical division. The latter, which was for the church in particular, involved matters of church organization, order, discipline, and government. According to Scott's schematization, these three divisions encompassed all the truths concerning Jesus Christ, salvation, and the church. Although Scott wrote about each of these divisions, the primary focus of his preaching and theological writings was on the first two divisions — the evangelical and transitional. The proposition regarding Jesus Christ as the Messiah, the evidences from Scripture supporting it, the process of salvation, and baptism were the most crucial issues for him. Thus, the truth that Jesus Christ is Messiah was Scott's point of departure for interpreting the whole of Scripture and all the doctrines that are encompassed by the Christian faith.

Footnotes

1. Scott made references especially to James Macknight, Joseph Lomas Towers, and Sir Isaac Newton.

2. Scott, *The Gospel Restored*, p. 65, quoted Locke on this point: "He that takes away Reason to make way for Revelation puts out the light of both; and does much about the same as if he would persuade a man to put out his eyes, the better to receive the remote light of an invisible star by a telescope." (Locke: *An Essay Concerning Human Understanding*, bk. 4, ch. 19.4).

3. Henry Lord Brougham, *A Discourse of Natural Theology, Showing the Nature of the Evidence and the Advantages of the Study* (Philadelphia: Carey, Lea, and Blanchard, 1836).

4. Scott, *The Gospel Restored*, pp. 60-67.

5. This is the conclusion Brougham reached regarding the relationship between natural and revealed theology. His argument for natural theology and its validity was based not on specific passages of Scripture but on the exercise of human reason and an inductive examination of the works of nature. To support his position he referred to Newton, Bacon, Butler, Boyle, Paley, and Clarke, who also advocated this approach to the question of natural and revealed theology.

6. Scott, *The Gospel Restored*, p. 66. See also, Scott, *The Messiahship*, pp. 15-16.

7. Scott, *The Gospel Restored*, pp. 233-234.

8. The theory that the Scriptures were literally inspired and inerrant was advocated by some of the ablest biblical scholars in England and Scotland in the eighteenth and nineteenth centuries. Many of these biblical interpreters, who influenced Scott's understanding and interpretation of the Scriptures, employed the grammatico-historical method that was based on Baconian induction.

9. Scott, *The Messiahship*, pp. 5-174.

10. Scott, *The Gospel Restored*, p. 323.

11. Ibid., pp. 259-260.

12. Scott, *A Discourse on the Holy Spirit*, p. 3.

13. Scott, *The Gospel Restored*, pp. 522-523.

14. Scott, *A Discourse on the Holy Spirit*, pp. 14-19. See also Scott, *To Themelion*, pp. 18,25.

15. Scott, *A Discourse on the Holy Spirit*, p. 6.

16. Ibid., pp. 14-15.

17. Ibid., pp. 20-21.

18. Scott, *To Themelion*, pp. 8, 12, 16.

19. Scott, *The Gospel Restored*, pp. 133,135.

20. Scott, *The Messiahship*, p. 5. Cf. Scott, *To Themelion*, pp. 6,17,19.

21. Scott, "Address: given before the American Christian Missionary Society," *Report of Proceedings of the Convention of Churches of Christ, at the Anniversaries of the American Christian Bible, Missionary, and Publication Societies, Held in Cincinnati, October 17th, 18th, 19th, and 20th, 1854. Prepared for Publication by the Secretaries* (Cincinnati: American Christian Publication Society, T. Wrightson & Co., printers, 1854), p. 26.

22. Scott, *The Gospel Restored*, p. 220.

23. J.J. Haley, *Makers and Molders of the Reformation Movement*, with an Introduction by J.H. Garrison (St. Louis: Christian Board of Publication, 1914), p. 68.

24. Scott, *The Messiahship*, pp. 259-260.

25. Ibid., pp. 260-261.

26. Ibid., p. 17.

27. Ibid., pp. 175-253.

28. Ibid., pp. 23-27.

29. Ibid., pp. 30-31, 176, 252.

30. Scott viewed these Old Testament prophecies as having been given verbally to the prophets by the Holy Spirit and literally foretelling events in the life of Christ.

31. Ibid., pp. 219-232. Scott referred to numerous passages in the Old Testament that predicted the incarnation: Psa. 2:7-8; Isa. 7:14; 9:6-7; Jer. 31:32; 33:15; and Zech. 13:7.

32. Ibid., p. 231.

33. Ibid., p. 220.

34. Luke 1; John 1; Rom. 1; I Tim. 3:16.

35. Ibid., p. 226.

36. Ibid., pp. 232-242. Scott referred to numerous passages in the New Testament concerning the initiation of the messianic mission at the Jordan River, but he focused mainly on the reports in the four Gospels: Matt. 3; Mark 1; Luke 3; and John 1.

37. In Scott's thinking the anointing of kings and high priests was a type of the anointing of Jesus with the Holy Spirit at His baptism. His installation into the office of Messiah was prophesied in the Old Testament: Isa. 40:10; 54:13; 61:1; and Jer. 31:31-34. On these particular prophecies and their meaning, Scott stated: "From the above prophetic notices we deduce the following, namely, that the eternal God was to be present at the inauguration of the Messiah, to give him at that solemn crisis, the spirit of his office without measure, and introduce the people to him in the glorious words, 'My Son,' etc." (Ibid., p. 235).

38. Ibid., p. 233.

39. Ibid., pp. 243-253. Although the transfiguration was not foretold by the Old Testament prophets, it was a miracle prophesied by

COME NOW, LET US REASON TOGETHER

Christ Himself, as Scott explained: "Touching the Transfiguration, ancient prophecy is silent on the subject. It was a display of power intended, at the juncture, to meet a particular exigence in the Apostolate and conserve its unity and integrity. Yet our Lord being a minister of the circumcision and a Jewish prophet, did foretell it before it occurred; and therefore, like the other miracles in the basis of his Messiahship, it was of a composite character — a miracle of prophecy as well as of power. 'Verily I say unto you, there are some standing here that shall not taste death until they see the kingdom of God come with power.' " (Ibid., p. 243).

40. Ibid., p. 247.
41. Ibid., pp. 175-183. See also Scott, *He Nekrosis*, where he discussed at some length the death and atoning work of Christ.
42. Scott, *The Messiahship*, p. 181.
43. Scott, *He Nekrosis*, pp. 23-25.
44. Ibid., p. 25.
45. Scott, *The Messiahship*, p. 177.
46. Scott, *He Nekrosis*, pp. 10-11. To support these ideas he referred to John 10:14-15; I Pet. 2:21-25; and Heb. 2, 9, 10.
47. Scott, *He Nekrosis*, p. 71.
48. Ibid., pp. 21-22.
49. Ibid., pp. 39, 55, 74.
50. Ibid., p. 60.
51. Ibid., pp. 66-67. See also Scott, *The Gospel Restored*, p. 515.
52. Scott, *The Gospel Restored*, p. 84.
53. Ibid., p. 513.
54. Scott, *The Messiahship*, pp. 342-343.
55. Scott, *He Nekrosis*, p. 14.
56. Scott, *The Gospel Restored*, p. 549.
57. Scott, *The Messiahship*, pp. 179-180.
58. Scott, *The Gospel Restored*, p. 190.
59. Scott, *The Messiahship*, p. 184. See Ibid., pp. 184-202, for his discussion of the meaning of the resurrection.
60. Psa. 2:7-11; 16:8-11; and Isa. 53:10.
61. Ibid., p. 202.
62. Ibid., pp. 185-186.
63. Ibid., p. 186.
64. Ibid., pp. 202-209.
65. Ibid., pp. 210-218.
66. Ibid., pp. 202, 203, 208. Scott mentioned that Aaron ascending into the holiest of all was a type of Christ's ascension to heaven. Also, there was the translation to heaven of Enoch and Elijah prior to Christ's ascension. In the Old Testament the ascension of Christ was prophesied. Psa. 2:6-8; 16:11; and 68:18.

67. Ibid., p. 208.
68. Psa. 16:11; 21:1-7; and 110:4.
69. Ibid., pp. 210, 218.
70. Scott, *To Themelion*, pp. 26, 27, 33.
71. Scott, *The Messiahship*, pp. 5, 273; and Scott, *To Themelion*, p. 4.
72. Scott, *The Messiahship*, pp. 270-278.
73. Ibid., p. 278.
74. Scott, "Personal Notebook," pp. 257, 263; and Scott, *The Messiahship*, pp. 7, 75.

CHAPTER FOUR

WHAT MUST I DO TO BE SAVED?

The agents or preachers may be many — the instrumentality must be one — the gospel working faith and working by faith. Christ personal, then, is the remote cause, and Christ preached the immediate cause, or the instrumentality, in regeneration.

Walter Scott, *The Messiahship*, p. 42.

The divinity of the Redeemer is the condition of Christian faith. Without something proved, we cannot believe. It is the common source of all the first principles of the kingdom of God. Faith, repentance, obedience, the remission of sins, and the gift of the Holy Spirit, are all discovered to us through the medium of this constitutional truth.

Walter Scott, *To Themelion*, p. 33.

As the Christian ministers and evangelists attempted to win the souls of the frontiersmen for the cause of

Christ, they all agreed on certain fundamental truths of the faith. They believed that Jesus Christ is the Saviour and Lord of the church. Also, they preached that salvation meant a sense of peace and forgiveness of sins in the present. One would escape the wrath of God and have a heavenly home in the future.

Some of the frontier people were indifferent to the claims of religion; others embraced them heartily. Faith could come to them in many different ways, with varying degrees of human emotion involved. They differed also concerning how much effort the individual could contribute towards his or her salvation, or whether God had elected certain ones for salvation and others for eternal damnation.

One could almost imagine the kinds of conversations that took place. For example, one might well visualize a group of people around 1827 in a small town in northeastern Ohio, in the section called the Western Reserve. They were discussing their religion and the time of their conversion.

One man there related how he was converted through hearing James McGready preach. The first meeting of McGready's revival was held at the Gaspar River Church in Logan County, Kentucky, in July 1800. He explained, "McGready told us that we were all depraved, condemned sinners; we were damned and would be tormented forever in the fires of hell. God, however, had elected to save a portion of fallen humanity through Jesus Christ."

Someone nearby commented, "That sounds like good Calvinistic preaching to me. The Calvinists believe there is very little you can do to be saved, because God has already elected certain ones for salvation."

"Yes," he acknowledged, "but James McGready was a special kind of Calvinist; he was what they called a 'New Light Presbyterian.' McGready told us that only those persons who used the 'means of grace' would have the assurance of pardon."

"What did he say about the means of grace?" another questioned.

"Well," he explained, "we must mourn our lost state and cry out to God for pardon. We need to listen to the voice of our consciences and the stirring of the Holy Spirit within us. We should meditate on how full and free is the salvation that God grants. McGready told us that God most likely would work salvation in a person who was using the means of grace. You begin to feel the Holy Spirit moving in you, and he called this the 'awakening time.' The Holy Spirit convinces us that we cannot save ourselves; we struggle for salvation and cry out for mercy. Finally, conversion comes when we have a grand vision of the glory of God in the face of Jesus Christ. McGready preached that our hearts would be filled with the love of God who saves sinners. This love of God makes us willing and able to come freely to Christ for the forgiveness of our sins."

Someone standing nearby said, "So, McGready preached that even if everybody used the means of grace, only the elect would be saved."

The narrator responded, "That's what he seemed to say."

Another lady there told about attending the Cane Ridge Revival on August 7-11, 1801, where she was converted. As she narrated her experience, "There must have been somewhere between ten and twenty thousand people at the revival. They came from miles around — on foot, horseback, and wagon. It was like a great social occasion as they greeted each other, but most of the people came to 'get religion' or just hear good preaching. Lots of ministers were there — Baptists, Methodists, and Presbyterians. I remember hearing one of these preachers, Barton W. Stone. Sometimes these ministers were all preaching at the same time, day and night, for nearly a week. It was quite a sight to behold! At night the lanterns were glowing and the candles flickering, as the preachers all sought to save the lost. The doctrine these ministers preached was simple and nearly the same — free salvation for all people. There was not much talk about salvation only for the elect. They preached that Christ died for all people."

Someone in the group remarked, "It sounds like there was a lot of excitement at Cane Ridge."

"Oh, yes," she said, "Emotions were running high. You should have seen the 'exercises' at Cane Ridge. There were the falling, jerking, barking, dancing, laughing, running, and singing exercises. I saw one little girl struck down by the Spirit. Hundreds of people were lying on the ground like soldiers slain in a battle, apparently dead and breathless. Some were crying aloud for God's mercy, and others were singing songs of praise and rejoicing because they were saved."

A man listening to her intently exclaimed, "It looks as though the Holy Spirit was really at work saving the lost, almost like a nineteenth century Pentecost!"

The lady continued, "Yes, it was. I remember Barton Stone telling about the revival and all of this religious excitement. He said he didn't understand it, but the whole atmosphere of religion, exercises, and expressions of piety could be nothing other than the mysterious workings of God. Stone rejoiced in the great number of souls converted to the Christian faith and the fact that some of the slumbering saints were awakened. I recall Stone saying something that was very meaningful to all of us — that in the heat and emotions of the revival all of the sects seemed to be united in one body of Christian people."

A young girl engrossed by her account remarked, "That must have been quite a sight to behold!"

One other man in the group related his experience in hearing Walter Scott, as he was preaching in one of the churches of the Western Reserve: "Scott was different from James McGready and all of those preachers at the Cane Ridge Revival. His message was a clear and simple one. I didn't hear him say a thing about being totally depraved or God electing certain ones for salvation. What I remember quite clearly is that he quoted a lot of Scripture when he preached. Scott called on people to accept Jesus Christ as the Messiah and Son of God. Then he said that the steps to salvation were like pointing to the fingers on your hand — faith, repentance, baptism, remission of sins, and the gift of the Holy Spirit. It was all so reasonable and scriptural that I accepted Christ as my Lord and was baptized by Scott that very night."

Several of the people there were curious about Walter Scott and his preaching. "Tell us more," one of them asked. "Who was he, and what did he preach about salvation? His preaching is a lot different from what the

Calvinists tell us, and I was brought up on Calvinistic preaching."

This chapter, then, attempts to answer some of these queries and treat in some detail certain aspects of Scott's thought. More specifically, the discussion will center on the nature of humanity, the origin of salvation in Jesus Christ, and the steps one must take in the process of salvation according to God's new covenant with humanity.

Father Adam and His Children

One of Walter Scott's central concerns was preaching the gospel of Jesus Christ and the steps one must take in order to be saved. His understanding of salvation presupposed a certain view of the nature of humankind and human sinfulness. He formulated these ideas of human nature and the process of salvation over against the prevailing Calvinistic views. The way he discussed these themes bears the mark of a polemic. In developing his theology in opposition to Calvinism, Scott was strongly dependent upon the rationalistic perspective of John Locke, especially Locke's theory of human knowledge. According to Scott, the Scriptures describe humanity as having existed in three clearly defined and distinct states — the natural and preternatural states and the state of respite.

The natural state was the condition of Adam and Eve as they were created by God in His image and placed in the Garden of Eden, an historical place.[1] There they existed in a harmonious relationship with God (Gen. 1:27-31; 2:15). This condition before the fall was ordered and arranged according to the will of God, and for this reason could be considered divine.[2] In their natural state they were in possession of righteousness, happiness, and life.[3] The first couple in this habitat lived in a relationship of favor with God and were in a state of innocence.[4] By this, Scott meant that Adam and Eve had no knowledge or experience of death and would have lived forever if they had not sinned. Pain, misery, and guilt lay totally beyond their state of innocence and were consequently non-existent. In this state of innocence and perfection, the first pair lived in the Garden of Eden for probably at least one hundred years.[5]

In the Garden, Adam was admitted to personal and sensible fellowship with God. In this interpretation of Adam and his knowledge of God, Scott was viewing him from a predominantly Lockean perspective, that is, that our knowledge comes from experience: sensation and reflection.[6] Since Adam had this direct, sensible knowledge of God, he did not need to exercise faith, as Scott explained:

> He had, by his original condition, been honored with knowledge . . . , and was consequently never called to walk by faith in regard to the divine existence. He did not believe that there was a God, he knew that there was a God. In his primitive state he was admitted to face-to-face intercourse and heard his voice; what a man sees and hears, therefore, he knows rather than believes, belief being referable to the experience of others, knowledge to the experience of one self. . . . Consequently he was the first person on earth whose apprehension of the divine existence was not derived from the testimony of others.[7]

Following the preternatural state and state of respite, at the return of the Messiah in the millennium, those who are pure in heart and belong to Him, will be permitted to see God face to face and have sensible fellowship with Him such as Adam had.[8]

The second state of humanity, which originated with Satan, was an evil one and was designated by Scott as preternatural. In essence, the preternatural state was that condition into which Adam and Eve were thrust as a result of the temptation and fall.[9] The sin of the original pair was an act of disobedience to God, their own voluntary act of the will.[10] In his interpretation of the fall, Scott followed Locke, who saw it as a loss of immortality and the beginning of death.[11] As a result of this original sinful act, Scott viewed the fall as fatal and deadly and having grave consequences. Adam and Eve experienced a radical change of state. From a condition of life, righteousness, and happiness, they entered into a state of guilt, misery, cowardice, shame, and death.[12] Scott summed up the results of the fall and the preternatural state of Adam and Eve:

> In the fall the glory departed; sin usurped the place of righteousness; death, of life; and the sorrows of earth, the pleasures of Eden. By the law of genus and species, therefore, the race were accounted:
> 1. Sinners.
> 2. Adjudicated to death.
> 3. And bereft of the Paradisaical state.
> Hence, since the fatal era of the fall of man, these sore evils have haunted our common humanity; sooner or later they are verified in the experience of every man.[13]

Regarding this preternatural condition and what Adam and Eve themselves experienced, Scott wrote elsewhere that "they felt they were naked; they felt they were in their persons defenseless, ignorant of death, afraid to meet it, and incapable of either resisting, or escaping it."[14]

Adam and Eve were so constituted that even in the Garden prior to the fall, they were capable of sinning and experiencing death.[15] Important for Scott, as with Locke, was that through the disobedient act of Adam and Eve death become a reality. When they sinned the whole race sinned in the sense that death entered, and the whole race was condemned to die. On this the Apostle Paul wrote: "Therefore as sin came into the world through one man and death through sin, and so death spread to all men because all men sinned" (Rom. 5:12). Scott's view was that through the fall the human state was changed from good to evil and life to death. In this context, Scott was referring to the death of the physical body; yet, in this whole process he insisted that the essential nature of humanity remains unchanged. The sin of Adam and Eve, therefore, accounted not only for their own death but also the death of all persons who have followed. The human race is a sinful one, born out of communion with God, and exists under the wrath of God because of this primal adjudication to death.[16]

Although Scott held these views regarding the reality of death and human sinfulness, he did not espouse the orthodox Calvinistic ideas of original sin and total depravity.[17] The human race is sinful, not only because death entered when Adam sinned, but in the further sense that all persons inevitably sin. Even at this, persons are not totally depraved, since they are capable of reasoning and exercising their capacity for faith. Original sin refers only to the sin of Adam and Eve; there is no inherited guilt passed on through the race as is stressed in the Calvinistic scheme.[18]

The state of respite, the third state of humankind, had its origin in the mercy of God, and for this reason can be called a divine one like the natural state. Following the fall, God inaugurated a new era of grace whereby persons can be regenerated.[19] The whole history of salvation has been God's efforts to redeem humankind from the state of sin and condemnation and grant eternal life. During this time revealed religion and the church have been given as the means by which persons can be saved. The opportunity to exercise faith and enter the church has been granted to humanity as a possibility. Regarding the present state of respite and what it entailed, Scott wrote:

> The state of respite is so named, because in it man is vouchsafed a respite for life, the present life. It is of a mixed nature partaking of both good and evil; it is inferior to the first or natural state, and superior to the second or preternatural state; it possesses neither the goods of the former, nor the evils of the latter; it is a condition in which man may either improve, or abuse, the life which has been lent him by his good, and wise, and all-benevolent Creator. Revealed religion is the means by which he may improve life, and become what God would have him to be; and to condemn or reject this, is to insult God and abuse the life which he has lent us.[20]

Whereas in the natural state Adam and Eve had direct knowledge of God, in the present state of respite humanity is bereft of this sensible knowledge of and communion with God. In the fallen state humankind has depended for knowledge of God on reason, experience, and the testimony of others. Hence, what knowl-

edge of God humanity now has is possessed only
through faith.

> Man's mental acquisition by his own experience is
> called knowledge, his acquisition by the experience of
> others is styled faith, the total of his acquisitions, there-
> fore, consists of knowledge and faith. What man knew
> of the existence of the Deity in his natural state, was
> knowledge; in the present state of respite, it is faith. . . .
> When, therefore, man fell from his natural condition,
> knowledge yielded to faith, and a state of things, in
> which man knew there was a God, was bartered away
> for that out of which he could be delivered only by the
> principle of believing that there is a God. Instead of
> enjoying his own experience on this point, he has now
> to trust to the experience of others, that is, he has to
> depend on particular revelations granted through the
> ministrations of particular men, as Adam, Enoch, Abra-
> ham, Moses, David, Isaiah, Malachi, John the Baptist,
> and our Lord and Saviour, who declares, that he had
> seen the Father. Meantime, faith is the only remaining
> organ of communion with God, found in the constitu-
> tion of man.[21]

By saying that knowledge of God in the present comes
through faith, Scott did not intend to negate what he
had stated regarding natural theology and knowledge
of God through the exercise of human reasoning, as in
Locke and Brougham. His emphasis, however, was
directed primarily towards the knowledge of God that
comes from the revelation in Scripture and the acceptance of this testimony by faith. Scott could say, then,
that knowledge of God comes through faith. In his
understanding of the knowledge of God in both the natural state and the state of respite, the controlling principle was Locke's idea of knowledge by experience
(sensation and reflection) and a rejection of all innate

ideas (Descartes). Scott was referring to Locke's principles when he wrote:

> Man has not been left to originate the idea of God; for he can originate no idea whatever, but is so constituted that things must originate in him their own ideas. God has, therefore, implanted his own idea in him by a sensible discovery of himself in person to one, Adam, and by a rational manifestation of his glorious works to all, which are greatly illustrative and confirmatory of the traditional testimony.[22]

Behold, I Will Make a New Covenant

In his understanding of the salvation of humankind from the fallen state, Scott used the biblical ideas of covenants, dispensations, and election as a framework for his thought. We have noted previously that Scott followed Locke very closely in his use of the idea of the biblical covenants and also that he was influenced by the covenant theology pervasive in the Church of England and Church of Scotland in the eighteenth century. Although Scott was subject to these influences, his formulation of these particular biblical ideas and the use he made of them in his theology were distinctive. Scott stressed to a greater degree than Locke the centrality of the covenant with Abraham and its significance for the biblical idea of election, which he placed over against the Calvinistic idea of God's eternal decrees in election. Also, the covenant idea, which he understood as a contractual agreement between two parties, underlay his conceptualization of the process of salvation: what God has done and what the individual must do.

According to Scott, there have been four ages or dispensations in the history of salvation and God's acts to redeem humankind: the Adamic, Patriarchal, Jewish, and Christian. Each of the dispensations centered around a revelation and a covenant made with a particular person: Adam, Abraham, Moses, and Jesus Christ. Although these dispensations differed in terms of the nature of the covenants governing them, in two fundamental points they were the same: there was one living God, and from Abel on, this proposition has been a matter of faith and not knowledge.[23] Concerning the proposition on belief in one God and what it encompasses Scott wrote:

> There are, as we have seen, two ways by which men can be assured of the divine existence, knowledge and belief. To Adam, it was a matter of knowledge; to other men it is a matter of belief. Hence the importance of the principle of belief in revealed religion, the fundamental idea of which is the being or existence of the Deity. The next is that of his Divine character, as the creator, preserver, and governor of the universe. In every dispensation of religion, therefore, whether Patriarchal, Jewish, or Christian, the divine character and divine existence have been indispensable, as facts to be believed.[24]

In his understanding of the biblical idea of election, Scott located its beginning not with the Exodus from Egypt but with the covenant made with Abraham.[25] It was the beginning or "Magna Charta" of the whole elect institution, and Abraham was the first elect person.[26] The principal thrust of Scott's argument on election was the relationship between Abraham and Christ (Gal. 3-4). His concern was with the blessings promised to Abraham, and by this he meant principally being of the elect and receiving salvation. He also saw the covenant with Abraham as the basis from which the covenants with Moses and Christ were derived in time. The guiding principles for his understanding of these latter two covenants were the election of persons to salvation and the basis upon which election was to be granted under these covenants.

Although Scott pointed out how the covenant with Moses was established, it did not figure as prominently as the covenants with Abraham and Christ. With Paul, Scott saw the Mosaic law as temporary and a custodian until Christ came (Gal. 3:25-28). The covenant with Moses admitted those of Jewish descent to the elect institution on the basis of circumcision and obedience to the law. According to Scott, Abraham and Christ are the primary elect persons, and it is either in Abraham or Christ that the blessings of salvation are obtained. Persons must be related to either of them according to certain principles before they are of the elect. By flesh (circumcision) the Jewish people belong to Abraham, and through faith they belong to Christ and receive the remission of sins.[27] The elect institution begun with Abraham culminated with the coming of Christ, and it will terminate at the millennium when all the gracious purposes of God are accomplished.

Scott's conception of election beginning with Abraham and continuing to Jesus Christ was a polemic against the Calvinistic idea of the divine decrees from all eternity, whereby individuals are elected either to salvation or damnation. Over against the Calvinistic scheme, which conceived the individual as a passive agent to be acted upon by the Holy Spirit in conversion,

Scott advanced the Enlightenment rationalistic conception of the autonomous individual. He placed emphasis on one's active role in conversion by exercising the capacity for faith. Scott expressed in strong terms his opposition to Calvinism:

> The Apostles never preached election to unconverted people as the Calvinists do; and the disciples themselves were never spoken to on this matter as persons who had believed, because they were elected, but rather as those who were elected because they had believed. . . . [28]

He continued his attack on Calvinism:

> Calvinistic election exhibits the divine sovereignty in a point in which it by no means obtains in Christianity. It is not exhibited in a capricious choice of this, that, and other persons, and passing by others, as Calvinism would and does have it; but in the justification of sinners of all nations on the principle of faith, as will appear by and by, an act of God's sovereignty, which was very displeasing to the Jews.[29]

In Scott's understanding of the Christian dispensation, the covenant idea was fundamental. His formulation of the gospel and the means to salvation were set within the context of the covenant principle: what God has done and what sinners must do in order to be saved.[30] It was this conceptual framework that underlay his idea of Jesus Christ as the Messiah and Son of God (the Golden Oracle) and the six steps involved sequentially in the process of salvation (Matt. 16:6 and Acts 2:38). On this covenant principle and what was entailed in it Scott wrote:

> The gospel is, primarily, a rational advocacy. It pleads the faith in its saving proposition from evidence. It is

133

secondarily a moral advocacy from what God has done for us to what we must do for ourselves. He has given us the truth and the proof; we must believe for ourselves. As in nature, he gives us the sun, the seed, and the soil, and leaves us to sow, reap, and gather for ourselves, so in religion, he presents us with truths, facts, commands, promises, but we must believe, repent, and obey for ourselves.[31]

The Salvation of Humanity: Jesus Christ and the Gospel Preached

Although Scott followed Locke very closely in his understanding of the gospel and the means to salvation, there were differences in their emphases. Scott went beyond Locke in establishing a pattern of salvation involving six steps in sequence. Especially important for Scott was the fact that the remission of sins, gift of the Holy Spirit, and promise of eternal life follow baptism; these latter elements were not emphasized as strongly by Locke as by Scott. His view of the Christian faith and salvation entailed a predominantly rational interpretation of the Scriptures and was formulated to counter the prevailing Calvinistic theology preached on the American frontier. The crucial issues involved in Scott's polemic against Calvinism centered on the role of the Holy Spirit in conversion, the nature of the human response to the gospel, and the sequence of steps in the process of salvation.

Scott differentiated between the first or mediate cause of regeneration and the immediate or instrumental cause. Jesus Christ, the regenerative head of the human race, is the first and real cause; the salvation of humankind originated with Him and His atoning death. The immediate or proximate cause of regeneration is the preaching of the gospel of Jesus Christ by the apostles and subsequent preachers.[32] For Scott, the gospel is the presentation of Jesus Christ as the Messiah based on the evidences of prophecy fulfilled and the miracles performed on him. The regeneration of the individual through the gospel involves six steps: faith, repentance, baptism, remission of sins, gift of the Holy Spirit, and the promise of eternal life. Scott summed up his ideas of these two closely related causes, the first and immediate:

> What, then, is the immediate, the instrumental cause by which he regenerates the heart and transfigures all the purposes of the soul and spirit? . . . It is by the gospel, then, in Scripture styled "the word," "the word of life," "the word of truth," . . . This has been, is now, and ever will be the exclusive instrumentality, whether the agent that speaks it be God, or Christ, or the Holy Spirit, or the holy apostles, or the Church, or her ministry: The agents or preachers may be many — the instrumentality must be one — the gospel working faith and working by faith. . . .
> Christ personal, then, is the remote cause, and Christ preached the immediate cause, or the instrumentality, in regeneration.[33]

Scott conceived salvation as a regeneration and a new birth,[34] whereby sin is eradicated from one's life. When the gospel is preached, the individual is able to weigh the evidences regarding Jesus Christ as the Messiah and make a response in faith and repentance, apart from a special mysterious operation of the Holy Spirit on the soul. Through faith and repentance the individual experiences regeneration and a moral transformation. In baptism one receives the remission of sins and is translated from the world to the church. Following baptism is the gift of the Holy Spirit and the promise of eternal life. Through the Spirit one's soul is changed to a spiritual state. Thus, the regeneration and new birth of the individual is by "water and spirit" (John 3:5). Scott described this total change:

> When the preached gospel has regenerated a man, and the transitional ordinance has conveyed him from the world to the church, he is then born of water, and stands to God in the relation of a son; here the Holy Spirit of God meets him as such, and by a spiritual operation, understood only by its effects, changes the state of his soul from the negative to the positive of spiritual life. Here Spirit meets spirit, the divine the human, and the convert is endowed with "power, love, and a sound mind". . . .
> Thus the regenerated is changed by water and the Spirit in the state, both of his soul and his body — and is thence called a new creature.[35]

Calvinism Opposed: Beecher and Doddridge

One of the crucial issues in which Scott's theology diverged from that of orthodox Calvinism focused on the role of the Holy Spirit in conversion. As examples of the theology of the Calvinists, Scott referred specifically to the views of Lyman Beecher and Philip Doddridge.[36] According to their views, it is necessary for the Holy Spirit to exert a special influence on the soul of the individual, regenerating it and enlightening the mind so that one can believe the gospel. The work of the Holy

Spirit, then, is first in the process of salvation, following which the individual exercises faith.

Scott opposed the views of Beecher and Doddridge for two reasons, both of which centered around their interpretations of the Holy Spirit. First, he argued that their conception of salvation is intended to state and defend the position of orthodox Calvinism as expressed in their standard confessions, and no scriptural passages concerning the role of the Holy Spirit are mentioned. Second, according to their Calvinistic theological orientation, the Holy Spirit is given to the elect at the beginning of the process of salvation to bring about regeneration and faith. Scott, as opposed to Beecher and Doddridge, believed that the Holy Spirit is imparted to the individual following baptism (Acts 2:38). Scott's position was that the autonomous individual can believe the evidences in Scripture regarding Jesus Christ and exercise faith apart from the inner workings of the Holy Spirit in regeneration.[37] For Scott, then, the instrumental cause of salvation is the gospel preached; for Beecher and Doddridge it is the Holy Spirit. In essence what was involved in Scott's attack on Beecher and Doddridge was the Calvinistic theological perspective, as expressed in the Westminster Confession of Faith,[38] over against his Enlightenment philosophical orientation (Bacon and Locke) and his method of biblical rationalism.

Steps in the Process of Salvation: Faith and Repentance

Walter Scott, in his preaching and writing, understood the salvation of humanity in terms of the new covenant given by God, which entailed truths, facts, commands, and promises. From the perspective of the individual, the covenant necessitated six steps in sequence — three things the individual must do, followed by God's promise to do three things in response. In this process, according to him, the first two steps are faith and repentance, the priority being given to faith, in that belief in Jesus Christ as the Messiah (the Golden Oracle) produces repentance.

For Scott, faith is an innate human capacity, an organ of knowledge given by God; one may exercise faith apart from the inner working of the Holy Spirit. It entails believing the testimony of others and availing oneself of the experiences they were reporting.[39] In his understanding of knowledge and faith, Scott followed Locke closely in conceiving all knowledge as coming from experience, i.e., observation (sensation) and reflection. The biblical writers, the prophets and apostles, experienced sensually the message or revelation from God and recorded it in the writings that have become Scripture. According to Scott, individuals are able to appropriate this knowledge, and this appropriation of the testimony of others or believing the evidences in Scripture is faith (Heb. 11:1-3). Hence, Scott could say that "the mental acquisition we make by the experience of others is called faith."[40]

Faith as a state of mind consists of two elements: belief and trust. Applied to the Scriptures, faith means not only believing in the validity of the testimony of others but also trusting and having confidence in what they expressed in their writings.[41] The element of belief

and trust or confidence applies in a more personal way
to God and Jesus Christ. One believes in the existence of
God and in the proposition regarding the messiahship
of Jesus Christ. On a deeper note, however, faith implies
trust in God and his promises. One goes beyond giving
intellectual assent to the messiahship of Jesus Christ
and trusts in Him as Saviour and relies confidently on
His words and the religion He established. Thus, faith
entails both intellectual and personal components:

> The apostle defines faith, in general, to be "the confi-
> dence of things hoped for, the evidence of things not
> seen"; of course Christian faith, in particular, must be an
> assent to the evidence of the existence of the Messiah,
> though we do not see him, and a confident reliance on
> God as one who means what he says, and who will per-
> form what he has promised. Thus true belief engages
> both the head and heart of a man . . . many now have
> only the one half of the true faith, and believe that
> Christ exists, without having the least confidence in
> either him, his words, or his institutions.[42]

Subsequent to faith and intimately related to it in the
process of salvation is repentance.[43] In order to understand Scott, it is necessary to see faith and repentance in
relation to the condition of sinful humanity or the state
of respite and how sin is overcome. For him sin is primarily disobedience to God's law involving one's
speech and conduct. Because of these acts of disobedience to the laws of God, humanity is corrupt; guilt,
shame, unrighteousness, and death characterize the present state of humankind. Sin is a "fibrous root,"[44] affect-
ing all humanity, and this love of sin in the mind and
practice must be destroyed, especially by faith in Jesus
Christ as the Messiah and by repentance.

In Scott's thinking, faith means believing the scriptural evidences regarding God and Jesus Christ and trusting in them. One believes in the teachings of Christ concerning the way of salvation and the good life. Faith as intellectual assent to the evidences and trusting in them, therefore, entails an enlightenment and change in the mind, a clarification of one's religious ideas. Through reflecting on the objects of faith (God, Jesus Christ as Messiah, and his teachings on the way of salvation), a moral change occurs in the mind; this change of mind and heart, which is expressed in outward conduct, is called repentance. Scott explained:

> Things thus examined and reflected upon, have the power of affecting the mind and of changing its conditions both intellectually and morally, both in regard to its views and its feelings. When, therefore, the things of religion take such a permanent intellectual and moral effect on the mind as to affect both our sentiments and actions, it is called in scripture "metanoeo," a change of mind. This is the etymological and primary import of the Greek term translated repentance. . . .
> This is the sense in which it is frequently used in the New Testament; so that in the sacred oracles it has all the force of the English word "reformation." Now there is a substantial reason for this, too; because a change of mind, even for the better, is of but small value unless it gives birth to a change of manners; and, therefore, the word is understood in its best and most comprehensive meaning when it is understood to signify a renovation of both mind and conduct effected by the objects of our faith deposited in the mind and acting deeply and permanently on both the understanding, will, and affections.[45]

Repentance as a moral reformation and renovation of the self is expressed in one's obedience to Christ's teachings and a change in one's manner of life through generosity, liberality, charity, good faith, honor, honesty, and contentment.[46] In Scott's understanding of the Scriptures, therefore, faith issues in repentance, and the love and practice of sin are destroyed in one's life.[47]

Baptism for the Remission of Sins

For Scott, one of the central theological concepts and the focal point in the process of salvation is the ordinance of baptism. In the sequence of steps involved in this process, faith and repentance issue in a public confession of Jesus Christ as the Messiah and baptism in obedience to the demands of the gospel.[48]

Scott, along with Alexander Campbell and the other Reformers, stressed that baptism is a remitting ordinance for adult believers only, all views of infant baptism being excluded. The mode of baptism, according to the Scriptures, is not sprinkling or pouring but immersion or "dipping."[49] Scott was especially opposed to the widely practiced baptism of infants among the Catholics and certain Protestant groups, as it distorted the true meaning of baptism in the New Testament. Against these views he wrote:

> Who are to be baptized, or immersed, one who believes, or one who does not believe? The Catholics and the Protestants say, those who do not believe; that is, the infants of professed Christians are to be baptized. But of this the Scriptures are absolutely silent. There is not one word enjoining it on any person to baptize his children. The command is not baptize your children; but be yourself baptized for the remission of your sins. The com-

mission is not, he that is baptized and believes, but "he that believes and is baptized"; accordingly the apostles, the prophets, and evangelists, and first ministers of our religion, baptized only those who had previously believed the gospel. This leaves those who sprinkle children, wholly and absolutely without any scriptural authority for what they do, having neither example nor commandment for their human ordinance of infant baptism.[50]

Baptism is a transitional ordinance by which the regenerated person is translated from the world to the church.[51] From Scott's perspective, baptism is integrally related to faith and repentance, in that faith expresses itself in repentance and baptism. The key passage for Scott was Acts 2:38: "Repent, and be baptized every one of you in the name of Jesus Christ for the forgiveness of your sins; and you shall receive the gift of the Holy Spirit." Baptism is the culminating act of the penitent believer in obedience to Christ and the turning of the soul to God. Scott believed that baptism in and of itself apart from faith is void of significance; only in relationship to the believer's faith in Christ does it have genuine transitional and remitting power.[52]

In baptism the regenerated person receives the remission of sins, which Scott referred to as "justification."[53] The essential element involved in the remission of sins is not the act of baptism itself but the faith that finds expression in baptism as an act of obedience to the commands of Christ. Scott made this clear as he wrote:

Therefore although their sins were pardoned them in baptism, yet we are not allowed to think that they were pardoned for or on account of baptism; but on account of the faith which they had, and which had influenced

> them thus to accept it. . . . We are forgiven then, not
> because we are baptized, but because we need forgive-
> ness, and are by faith prepared to receive it through the
> merits of Christ alone.[54]

As Scott conceived it, there is no inherent merit or
cleansing power in the water of baptism itself. Jesus
Christ is the Saviour, and from Him and His atoning
death all saving power originates. Baptism is one of the
conditions put forth by Christ as the time and place
where the actual remission of sins can be realized.
Through faith and repentance one expresses trust in
Christ and the need for forgiveness. Baptism, then, is
the public act or expression of a person's state of mind
and heart; it is an acceptance of the promise of the
remission of sins offered in the gospel. Through baptism
Christ gives assurance of pardon to those who are obedient to Him and enter into covenant with Him.

If faith is the essential element in the remission of
sins, it is faith with a specific focus. One's faith is centered in Christ and especially His atoning blood.
According to Scott's penal substitutionary theory of the
atonement, the sins of all were borne by Christ in His
atoning death. To believe in Jesus Christ means to
believe in the atoning death by His blood and that this
atoning act is for the remission of sins. The Apostle Paul
makes this clear: "In him we have redemption through
his blood, the forgiveness of our trespasses, according to
the riches of his grace which he lavished upon us" (Eph.
1:7). Baptism, therefore, is the place where the penitent
sinner meets the atoning blood of Christ and receives
the remission of sins.[55] Thus, Scott could say that "the
blood of Christ . . . forms the real cause of pardon to all

who ever shall be forgiven."[56] In this same context, he also referred to baptism by faith in the blood of Christ as "the laver (bath) of regeneration."[57]

Scott's theology of baptism was formulated over against the idea of infant baptism (Presbyterians, Methodists, and Catholics) and the Baptist position. According to the thinking of the Baptists at this time, baptism is not intimately related to the remission of sins. It is an expression of loyalty to Christ after the penitent believer's sins are forgiven. In accordance with their Calvinistic theological orientation, the essential element in salvation is the experience of the Holy Spirit in regeneration. One was counseled to rely on feelings and the emotional state in the experience of regeneration as evidence of the forgiveness of sins. Scott opposed this viewpoint because it leaves the individual in a state of indefiniteness as to when one's sins are forgiven. If the Word of God is to be believed, as Scott urged, then one receives the assurance of pardon in the ordinance of baptism. God's plan of salvation, as revealed in the Scriptures, is that baptism is for the remission of sins by faith in the atoning blood of Jesus Christ, following which the Holy Spirit is given, and the soul is changed into a spiritual state. In his understanding and formulation of the doctrine of baptism, Scott also avoided the extreme position of baptismal regeneration, or "water salvation," as it was called. There is no saving power in the water as such or in the act of being immersed. Baptism by immersion in water is the outward expression of one's faith in Christ's atoning blood and obedience to the scriptural injunctions.

One final aspect of Scott's understanding of baptism

that needs to be noted is the relationship between baptism and the Trinity.[58] Scott understood the Godhead or Trinity as a revelation of the three divine persons: Father, Son, and Holy Spirit.[59] Although he admitted the validity of the Trinity as the true expression of the nature of God, a trinity in unity, he believed it is ultimately a mystery. He did not attempt to engage in speculation regarding the inner relationships of the persons of the Trinity or the modes of procession of the persons or hypostases as was characteristic of the Early Church. Because the Scriptures are silent on the nature of these inner relationships of the Trinity, it forms no essential part of the Christian faith.

Scott's interests centered mainly on using the trinitarian formula in baptism. Persons are baptized in the name of the Father, Son, and Holy Spirit because these three persons are involved in the revelation and very structure of the Christian faith; they are "the architects of our religion."[60] In Scott's thinking the Father declared the faith or messiahship (Jesus Christ as the Son of God) at the baptism of Jesus by John; this is the proposition to be proved. Jesus Christ revealed the doctrine, which includes all that He taught, especially the nature of salvation and the six steps involved. The proof of the proposition concerning the messiahship was given by the Holy Spirit in terms of the evidences of miracles and the fulfillment of prophecy. Scott expressed his views on baptism and the Trinity most clearly by writing:

> We are baptized into these names — to that of the Father first, because the faith precedes the doctrine; into that of the Son next, because the doctrine precedes the proof; and into that of the Spirit last, because the

volume of revelation is closed by the evidence. The reason of our baptism into the Trinity, then, is found in the relations of "faith," "doctrine," and "evidence" — the three elements constituting the framework of our religion.

. . . The Trinity is God revealed in his relations to redemption — God in his relations to the human, to the finite, the created, the temporary. This Trinity, then, is not designed to aid us in comprehending "one God," which is impossible; but to aid us in comprehending "one religion" — the Christian religion, which I have named "faith," "doctrine," and "evidence."[61]

Gift of the Holy Spirit and Promise of Eternal Life

In Scott's interpretation of the process of salvation, the final two steps are the gift of the Holy Spirit and the promise of eternal life. He emphasized in all of his writings and in preaching on salvation that the Holy Spirit is imparted to the believer subsequent to baptism for the remission of sins. All ideas of the Spirit as the first or primary cause of salvation, as expressed in Calvinistic theology, were opposed by Scott.[62] Because the Spirit is given only to those who have been translated from the world to the church in baptism and have become members of the body of Christ, it is a "missionary to the church."[63]

One of the central emphases in Scott's doctrine of baptism and gift of the Holy Spirit was the Johannine idea of being born of "water and spirit."[64] He appropriated these symbols of "water and spirit" in John 3:5 to represent the believer's entrance into two kingdoms. Through baptism in water one enters the kingdom on earth or the church, and through the gift of the Holy Spirit one is introduced to the kingdom of heaven.[65] When the individual receives the Holy Spirit and the soul is changed to a spiritual state, one is an inheritor of the kingdom of heaven, which will be experienced fully in the future. Scott further explained what he meant on the work of the Holy Spirit:

> It is said that we are born of the water, therefore, only because we proceed from it into the kingdom of God on earth; and born of Spirit only because we shall proceed from it at the resurrection and be ushered into the everlasting kingdom of heaven by its energies in raising us from the dead.[66]

Scott taught that following baptism the believer receives the gifts that the Holy Spirit bestows: comfort, soundness of mind, power, wisdom, and goodness.[67] The Spirit also becomes the connecting link between the members of the church and Christ as its head.[68] Because Jesus Christ is physically absent from the church through His resurrection and ascension, the Spirit makes up for His personal presence and becomes His substitute in the church.[69]

Life in the Spirit also entails the idea of internal evidences for the messiahship. The truth regarding Jesus Christ as the Messiah is, as has been emphasized, established on the basis of the scriptural evidences of miracles and prophecy fulfilled. In addition to these rational proofs for the truth of this central proposition of the Ancient Gospel, Scott utilized the conception of the inner witness of the Holy Spirit. The Spirit within the life of the believer gives special corroborating evidence for the truth of the messiahship. Scott expressed this most clearly in terms of objective proof and internal correlation for the messiahship:

> Its truth and authority rest on an objective or external proof; its wisdom and goodness on its subjective or internal correlation with our spiritual necessities.
>
> If a man would know this third phase of life, and enjoy it now and forever, he must not deal with Christianity arbitrarily, abstractly or theoretically, but place himself in a position in which he may feel the power of the forces of the kingdom of heaven, and participate in their benefits; then he will be able to judge 'experimentally' of the internal structure of our religion, and the wisdom of God who made it.[70]

Eternal life, as the sixth and final step in the process of salvation, is promised to all persons who fulfill the covenant conditions of faith, repentance, and baptism.[71] As Scott envisioned the relationship of the individual to eternal life, there is a twofold process. First, through the gift of the Holy Spirit the soul of the believer is changed to a spiritual state, and one enters the spiritual kingdom. Second, the promise of eternal life is to be realized in the future at the Second Coming of Christ and the resurrection of the dead.[72] Faith in God shall yield to direct personal and sensible knowledge of God, and persons shall be admitted into His presence. On the nature of the kingdoms, the earthly and the spiritual, and what they entail, Scott wrote:

> We have in the scriptures two kingdoms of Christ, one temporal in its duration, the other eternal; the former having in it earthly things or things to be enjoyed on earth, the latter, containing heavenly things or things which can be enjoyed only in heaven. These reigns are represented as differing in the following particulars

also, that the earthly things of the first are to be enjoyed
by faith; but that in the second faith is to give way to
knowledge and the heavenly things belonging to it shall
be enjoyed by absolute personal communion with them.
Here, the blessings are pardon and the Holy Spirit; but
in the everlasting kingdom they are eternal life and the
personal presence of God and the Lamb.[73]

Sometimes these two items, gift of the Holy Spirit and
promise of eternal life, were combined. Often in his
preaching Scott spoke only of the gift of the Holy Spirit.
When so combined, the meanings of both were
included. Taken together, it was implied that one grows
in grace and the Christian life and receives a promise of
the fulfillment of the Christian hope in life eternal.

Preaching a Saving Faith

Scott's method of biblical rationalism can be seen
clearly in his understanding of the Person of Jesus
Christ and in the way he formulated the plan of salvation. He called this the Ancient Gospel, and to him it
was like a long lost truth of Scripture he had rediscovered for his day. His interpretation of salvation was
strongly dependent on Locke's theory of knowledge
and was developed as a polemic against the Calvinistic
conception of salvation prevalent in the preaching on
the American frontier in the early nineteenth century.
Scott's view of salvation entailed six (sometimes five)
steps in sequence and was set within the context of the
covenant relationship. God has given truths, facts, commands, and promises. To fulfill the covenant, the individual is to do three things in order to be saved: believe,

repent, and be baptized. In response God saves the individual by remitting sins, giving the Holy Spirit, and promising eternal life. It was this understanding of salvation which Scott preached with such signal success on the Western Reserve from 1827-1830 and which pervaded his theological writings in the succeeding years. Most commonly it has been called simply the "five finger exercise."

Footnotes

1. Scott based his interpretation of Adam and Eve, their status in the Garden, and the subsequent temptation and fall on Gen. 1-3 and Rom. 5:12.

2. Scott, *The Gospel Restored*, pp. 9-10.

3. Ibid., p. 41.

4. Ibid., pp. 34-35.

5. Ibid., p. 21.

6. Scott's dependence on Locke's theory of human knowledge, especially regarding Adam, can be seen in the following statement: "When God formed man with the powers of sensation and reflection, he formed him with a capacity for knowledge; for this is that in which a capacity for knowledge consists — the power of acquiring ideas by sensation, and of reflecting upon them when acquired. Now these powers of sensation and reflection are bestowed upon all men, and, therefore, it is predicated of mankind universally, that they are everywhere endowed with a capacity for knowledge" (Ibid., p. 258).

7. Ibid., p. 55.

8. Ibid., pp. 11-12.

9. Ibid., pp. 9-10.

10. Ibid., pp. 31, 90. See also Scott, *He Nekrosis*, p. 5. According to Scott's literal interpretation of Gen. 2, the act of disobedience to the will of God was in eating from the tree of the knowledge of good and evil.

11. Locke, *The Reasonableness of Christianity*, sec. 1, pp. 1-6.

12. Scott, *The Gospel Restored*, pp. 39, 41, 43.

13. Scott, *The Messiahship*, p. 36.

14. Scott, *The Gospel Restored*, p. 19. See also pp. 34-35.

15. Ibid., p. 121.

16. Scott, *He Nekrosis*, p. 5.

17. Orthodox Calvinism saw Adam as the federal representative of the human race who acted on behalf of the future generations of humanity. Original sin refers to Adam's sin and the imputation of his sin and guilt to all humankind. Because all share in Adam's sin and guilt, all are involved in original sin, which consists in a corrupt nature, a sinful state, and the tendency to sin. In its doctrine of total depravity, orthodox Calvinism stressed that no aspect of humanity remains unaffected by the sin of Adam. One cannot take the first step towards salvation or deliver oneself from the state of sin. Only the elect can be regenerated by a mysterious inner action of the Holy Spirit.

18. Scott, *The Evangelist* 3 (July 1834): 151-153, engaged in a dialogue with an imaginary character, Jonathan. Scott argued that the doctrine of total depravity is nonscriptural and cannot form a legitimate topic of Christian conversation. His view was that all persons sin but are not totally depraved. All are created upright, yet transgress the law of God. Sin is a scriptural term but must be separated from the idea of total depravity. Likewise, Scott argued against the doctrine of original sin as being nonscriptural. It refers to the sin committed by our original parents; the rest of humankind cannot be deemed guilty because of their sin. Original sin is not passed on in a manner advocated by the Calvinists; persons are guilty only of the sins they commit. Since all are born into a sinful world and the conditions of sinful humanity, it is evident, however, that all persons will sin. Thus, Scott was attempting in this dialogue to maintain the reality of the Genesis account of Adam's fall as having serious consequences for all humanity, while at the same time avoiding the extreme positions of the Calvinists.

19. Scott, *The Messiahship*, p. 35.

20. Scott, *The Gospel Restored*, pp. 9-10.

21. Ibid., pp. 11-12. See also pp. 54-55.

22. Ibid., p. 56.

23. Ibid., pp. 54-57.

24. Ibid., p. 238.

25. In discussing the covenant with Abraham, Scott referred to Gen. 12:2-3; Neh. 9:7; Rom. 9-11; Gal. 3-4; Heb. 8; I Pet. 2:9-10; and II Pet. 1:10.

26. Ibid., p. 286. One may also refer to the series of articles Scott wrote in *The Christian Baptist* on the biblical idea of election. *The Christian Baptist*, ed. Alexander Campbell, 7 vols. (Buffaloe, Brooke County, Va.: printed and published by Alexander Campbell, 1827-1829; reprint. ed., Nashville, Tenn.: Gospel Advocate Company,

1955-1956). Walter Scott, "Election—No. I," *The Christian Baptist* 6 (March 1829): 177-179; "Election—No. II," *The Christian Baptist* 6 (May 1829): 240-243; "Election—No. III," *The Christian Baptist* 7 (October 1829): 69-73; and "Election—No. IV," *The Christian Baptist* 7 (October 1829): 73-77.

27. Scott, *The Gospel Restored*, pp. 282-286. See also Scott, "The Covenant. A Discourse," *The Evangelist*, n.s., 7 (August 1839): 169-184; and *The Christian* 1 (August 1837): 161-166.

28. Scott, *The Gospel Restored*, p. 280.

29. Ibid., p. 284.

30. He viewed the covenants in both the Old and New Testaments principally as contractual agreements formally binding God and humanity on the basis of certain principles. Although he saw the covenants in the Old Testament in relationship to the whole community of Israel, his main emphasis, especially in the covenant with Abraham, was the election of the individual to salvation. This focus on the individual is also seen in Scott's idea of the covenant in the New Testament. Here, his emphasis was on the salvation of the individual on the basis of the covenant relationship: what God has done and what the individual must do. In particular Scott focused on Matt. 3:17; 16:13-19; and Acts 2:38 as the basis of the covenant agreement. God has given to humanity Jesus Christ, the proofs in Scripture for the messiahship, and the teachings of Christ concerning salvation. He has thereby promised to remit sins, give the Holy Spirit, and grant eternal life to all who believe, repent, and are baptized.

31. Scott, *To Themelion*, pp. 78-79.

32. Scott, *The Messiahship*, pp. 40-41.

33. Ibid., pp. 41-42.

34. Ibid., p. 41.

35. Ibid., p. 44.

36. Scott, *The Gospel Restored*, pp. 425-445. His references were to Lyman Beecher, *Views in Theology, Published by Request of the Synod of Cincinnati*, 2nd. ed. (Cincinnati: published by Truman and Smith, 1836), pp. 197-229; and Philip Doddridge, *The Rise and Progress of Religion in the Soul: Illustrated in a course of Serious and Practical Addresses*, with an Introductory Essay, by John Foster (Boston: published by Perkins, Marvin, & Co., 1835), pp. 175-333. Scott's primary concern in referring to Beecher and Doddridge was to show how contemporary Calvinistic thinkers formulated the process of conversion. They represented a position over against which he was able to set his own ideas.

37. In his polemic against the Calvinistic understanding of salvation, Scott contended that faith is first in the process of conversion. It

comes through hearing the gospel preached, not by the inner action of the Holy Spirit. To make more pointed his views as opposed to the Calvinists, Scott distinguished between faith and inspiration: "If that state of mind which reposes with confidence in the testimony of another is described by the word faith or trust, this is a proof that 'Faith comes by hearing' as the apostle vouches. But now, if this state of mind were brought about by an operation of the Holy Spirit, as modern Christendom teaches, then the word which would have described it, is 'inspiration' and not 'fides'; and it would in Scripture be called inspiration and not belief. The apostolic commission also would have read, 'He who is inspired and is baptized, shall be saved; and he who is not inspired shall be damned', which indeed, is the very doctrine or down right absurdity, taught by the parties of the present day. Faith, then, human or divine, is trust or confidence in the testimony or experience of another." (Scott, *The Gospel Restored*, pp. 261-262).

38. In particular Scott was opposed to three articles in the Westminster Confession of Faith. See *Documents of the Christian Church*, 2nd. ed., selected and edited by Henry Bettenson (London: Oxford University Press, 1971), pp. 245-246:

"IX. Of Free Will. . . . Man, by his fall into a state of sin, hath wholly lost all ability of will to any spiritual good. . . . When God converts a sinner and translates him into the state of grace, He freeth him from his natural bondage under sin; and by His grace alone enables him freely to will and to do that which is spiritually good. . . .

"X. Of Effectual Calling. All those whom God hath predestinated unto life — and those only — He is pleased, in His appointed and accepted time, effectually to call by His Word and Spirit . . . not from anything foreseen in man, who is altogether passive therein. . . . Elect infants, dying in infancy, are regenerated and saved by Christ through the Spirit, who worketh when, where, and how He pleaseth. . . .

"XI. Of Justification. Those whom God effectually calleth, He also justifieth . . . by imputing the obedience and satisfaction of Christ unto them. . . . They are not justified, until the Holy Spirit doth in due time actually apply Christ unto them. . . . Although they can never fall from the state of justification, yet they may by their sins fall under God's fatherly displeasure. . . . "

39. Scott, *The Gospel Restored*, pp. 256-259. In his discussion of faith Scott referred primarily to Rom. 10:17 and Heb. 11:1-3.

40. Ibid., p. 260.

41. Ibid., pp. 260-261.

42. Ibid., pp. 287-288. See also Scott, *The Messiahship*, p. 22, where

he enunciated this conception of faith and stated that the proofs and evidences for faith are the bases for personal trust or inward faith: "Faith in him is not fiction but a valid conclusion — a great inference drawn by the human soul from all-sufficient premises laid down by the Holy Spirit in the Holy Scriptures. He claims no assent to the divinity of his mission from the say-so of priests, or the authority of sword or saber; or as its being the fruit of philosophy, or the offspring of mysticism, or of the human conscience, or human impulse of any kind; but instead offers outward argument for inward faith, and sustains proposition by proof."

43, In his discussion of repentance, Scott cited Mark 3:12 and Acts 2:38.

44. Scott, *The Gospel Restored*, p. 90.

45. Ibid., pp. 316-317.

46. Ibid., p. 317.

47. Ibid., p. 97.

48. Ibid., pp. 192-194, 256-257, 299, 317-318.

49. Scott, *The Messiahship*, p. 287; and Scott, *To Themelion*, pp. 82-92.

50. Scott, *The Gospel Restored*, pp. 474-475.

51. Ibid., pp. 98-99, 443-444; and Scott, *The Messiahship*, pp. 58-59.

52. In his discussion of baptism Scott quoted numerous passages of Scripture, all of which were interpreted to support his contention that it is a transitional ordinance in which the remission of sins is effected: Mark 16:16; John 3:5; Acts 2:38; 22:16; Rom. 6:3-4; Gal. 3:27; Col. 3:3; Titus 3:5; Heb. 10:22; I Pet. 3:21.

53. Scott, *The Gospel Restored*, pp. 290, 443-444.

54. Ibid., p. 299.

55. Scott, *He Nekrosis*, pp. 18, 57-58, 77, 84.

56. Scott, *The Gospel Restored*, p. 290.

57. *The Evangelist* 3 (March 1832): 61-62. Scott pointed to the close relationship between the blood of Christ and the remission of sins in the water of baptism: "Although Baptism was the time, place and ordinance in which God was pleased to impart forgiveness to the truly penitent, yet the blood of Christ was, in reality, the procuring cause of remission. How near to us has God brought the blood of Christ by the Christian Laver: nay, he has by this bath put us into the blood of Christ."

58. Scott, *The Messiahship*, pp. 270-284; and Scott, *To Themelion*, pp. 43, 97.

59. Scott, "Personal Notebook," p. 72.

60. Scott, *The Messiahship*, p. 281.

61. Ibid., pp. 283-284.

62. Scott, *A Discourse on the Holy Spirit*, pp. 3-4; Scott, *The Gospel*

Restored, pp. 97-99, 522, 528; and Scott, *He Nekrosis*, p. 39.

63. Scott, *The Gospel Restored*, p. 528; and Scott, *A Discourse on the Holy Spirit*, p. 3.

64. Scott, *The Messiahship*, pp. 43-45; and Scott, *The Gospel Restored*, pp. 553-559.

65. Ibid., p. 553.

66. Ibid., p. 559.

67. Ibid., pp. 407, 412, 43-440; and Scott, *A Discourse on the Holy Spirit*, p. 13. In his understanding of the gifts of the Spirit, Scott referred to John 14:16-18; 16:7-11; Acts 2:38; Rom. 8:15; I Cor. 12-13; and Gal. 5:22. He summed up his understanding of the gifts of the Spirit and what they entailed:

"1. The gifts of wisdom were, discerning of spirits, teaching prophecy, tongues, interpretation, knowledge, and all those gifts which enabled the apostles and others to understand the prophecies relative to the Messiah, and to recollect all things which the Saviour had told them on that subject when he showed them in the Law, the Prophets, and the Psalms, the things concerning himself.

"2. The gifts of power were those of miracles, healings, signs, and wonders, . . .

"3. The gifts of goodness were love, joy, gentleness, meekness, longsuffering, fidelity, . . . "

68. Scott, *The Messiahship*, p. 237.

69. Scott, *The Gospel Restored*, pp. 409, 418. In his understanding of the Person of Jesus Christ subsequent to the resurrection, Scott speaks from the perspective of Luke-Acts rather than Paul or John. Jesus Christ has ascended to heaven, is seated at the right hand of God, and is absent from the church. The mission of the Spirit is to be present to the church in place of or as a substitute for Christ. Hence, for Scott the believer has the gift of the Spirit and through Him experiences the presence of the risen Christ.

70. Scott, *The Messiahship*, pp. 261-262.

71. Scott, *The Gospel Restored*, p. 88.

72. See Scott, "Eternal Life: A Discourse of the Gospel," *The Evangelist*, n.s., 7 (February 1839): 25-48. Scott stated his ideas of eternal life here in terms of four propositions which are to be believed as part of the Ancient Gospel and the process of salvation:

"1. Eternal life is a matter of promise.

"2. Eternal life as promised to man is deposited with Christ in Heaven.

"3. Eternal life is the free gift of God.

"4. Eternal life, nevertheless, is conditional. The first condition is, that men believe in the Gospel, amend their lives, and be baptized. The second is, that they continue in well doing, or in the keep-

ing of the will of God til death." (Ibid., pp. 30, 41).
73. Scott, *The Gospel Restored*, p. 551.

CHAPTER FIVE

GOD'S OWN PEOPLE IN A HOLY NATION

Seeing God was pleased to foretell that he would create a new government and a new people, and seeing it was exceedingly proper to choose a "new world" to do it in, it may be that in the government and people of the United States we have an historical illustration of the grand prophecy, and that at home we are permitted to behold a change in government and society such as will finally obtain among all people.

Walter Scott, *The Messiahship*, pp. 321-322.

My poor wife is sitting by me, reading of Gen. Washington, and is as deeply affected by the state of our national affairs as I or any other person could be. This terrible affair has broken many a heart, and, I fear, if there is not a change for the better soon, it will break all hearts. I never heard of so grievous a case. Abundance of tears have been shed in my family this day over this sad event. It has torn me all to pieces. I thank the goodness

157

of God that civil war is not yet upon us. If all the Southern States secede without compromise, they will part from us in the worst spirit, and war will follow. Secession is war — Union, peace. I fear that, unless union is effected immediately, secession will reveal itself in the thunders of civil war.

Letter from Walter Scott to his eldest son, John,
early in 1861.

The Civil War was a watershed in American history, as the nation was rent asunder and bathed in blood. Swords clashed and cannons roared as the North and South fought long and hard. In this conflict and the years leading up to it, the principal issue was slavery. So crucial and invidious was slavery that Horace Bushnell, the Congregationalist minister, referred to the Civil War as an objective national atonement, a cleansing in blood for its corporate sin and guilt. Around the slavery question, which culminated in civil strife, were revealed the paradoxes of American history in the nineteenth century. The church itself was caught in these paradoxes and cross currents, and attempted to live its life and speak out on the burning questions of the day.

The first was that of freedom and slavery. The American Revolution of 1776 was fought to free the colonies from the oppression of the British crown. Thus, on July 8, 1776 the ringing of the Liberty Bell in Independence Hall, Philadelphia, heralded the signing of the Declaration of Independence four days earlier. This momentous event signaled that the colonies were free and independent of England and her yoke of oppression. The banner of liberty and human rights was held high by the colonists. With the turn of the century America was the land of the free, where persons could pursue their individual destinies and find fulfillment. Freedom was in the air people breathed. They were unlimited in their horizons and possibilities. True, it was a land of freedom, but unfortunately not all persons enjoyed this freedom. From the earliest days of settlement on the Atlantic seaboard, slavery was an American institution. Especially in the South it was a way of life and necessary for the economy. The Blacks did not enjoy this liberty others had, nor were they able to pursue happiness in their own way. Shackled in manacles and chains, they were auctioned off on the slave block to the highest bidder. Families were torn apart, and individuals were denied the basic freedoms provided in the Declaration of Independence and Constitution. It was not until the Civil War, the Emancipation Proclamation, and the Thirteenth Amendment to the Constitution that slavery was finally abolished in all states and territories of the United States. America was a land of freedom, but an uneasy freedom overshadowed by slavery.

Second, there was the paradox of unity and disunity. The War of Independence that brought the American nation into being united thirteen colonies into a federal union. One nation was forged in the fires of conflict. As the young nation grew and the church flourished, the Federal Government endeavored to preserve this union. The Constitution framed in 1787 became the law of the land and bound them into a unity. In the religious realm churches endeavored to form a basis upon which they could unite. This was true of the major denominations — Lutherans, Reformed, Protestant Episcopal, Presbyterians, and Congregationalists. The Christians and Disciples united in 1832 and attempted to forge a plan that would unite all Christian people. As the national unity remained intact and the churches endeavored to realize Christ's prayer "that they may all be one" (John 17:21), there were contrary winds blowing to threaten this unity. All of this centered around the question of slavery, a cancer that was eating away at the very fiber and tissue of the nation. The United States would soon polarize around the abolitionists and the proslavery forces. The fabric of the nation began to tear apart at the seams, leading finally to secession and the formation of the Confederacy. North and South both claimed the rightness of their cause over against the other and marshalled certain passages of Scripture to support their position. The issue of slavery and the Civil War would soon separate Black from White, Black from Black, and White from White, destroying thereby the unity of families and America itself. A nation of states united was feeling the winds of war that would fracture its unity, and a river of blood would course its way throughout the land.

The third paradox was the idea of America as God's chosen people, yet a people who were sinful and would soon experience the wrath of God. Since early days America was conceived as a nation with a Manifest Destiny. Its divinely appointed mission was to spread democratic government and Christian civilization throughout this land and to other nations. God had chosen this country, these people, for a mission — to create the kind of government and religion that would be an expression of his will. America was to be the arena for the coming Kingdom of God, the climax and fulfillment of all history. One could verily say that there was a messianic character to America, whose God-given task it was along with the church to usher in the millennial age. However, one may question the messianic character of a nation that had three and one half million persons in slavery. President Lincoln, in the "Second Inaugural Address," succinctly stated this paradox of God's chosen people as he expressed the destiny and present woes of the "almost chosen people." Lincoln went on in this "Address" and spoke of God's judgment against the evils of slavery in America. Being caught up in the delicate web of sectional self-interest, the South especially wanted to preserve a way of life and their economy, but at the expense of the dignity and denial of human rights to the Blacks in slavery. America was a nation that conceived itself as fulfilling the Almighty's will, a nation with a Manifest Destiny, yet a people who seemingly relegated to a secondary position the ideals of human rights, dignity, and freedom. For this sin, they would soon experience the judging hand of God.

These three paradoxes were present in mid-nineteenth century America, a nation on the brink of civil conflict. This was the era, these were the times, in which Walter Scott lived and preached and wrote. He felt deeply the tensions stemming from these paradoxes and agonized over the pressing concerns of the day, especially slavery. He did not live to experience the Civil War but did see it as a dark and foreboding cloud on the immediate horizon. What he thought and wrote about these crucial issues facing the nation and the church will be the subject of this chapter.

Rethinking the Church in a New Age

In the early and mid-nineteenth century in America, one of the crucial issues concerned the nature of the church, its mission, and how it should be structured.[1] More particularly, the inroads of pietism and rationalism and the widespread dependence upon the methods of revivalism had tended to erode traditional conceptions of the church. To a large extent American Christianity in the early decades of the nineteenth century was characterized by pluralism and a sectarian spirit. In order to meet this crisis and redefine the nature and purpose of the church, a number of different approaches were taken.

Some individuals representing various denominations responded by participating in voluntary benevolent societies for missionary activity, education, and reform. In this endeavor traditional theological differences were by-passed or ignored in the interest of finding unity in action. Certain groups of Baptists, Methodists, Congregationalists, and Presbyterians engaged in this enterprise and used revivalism as a means of spreading the gospel.[2]

Another response was on the part of certain denominations who reacted against voluntary benevolent activity, revivalism, sectarianism, and subjectivity in American Protestantism. Their answer to the situation facing the church was to reassert the older churchly traditions. In order to define more clearly the nature of the church some of the main denominations pointed to the objective, historical landmarks of the church. Emphasis was placed on creeds and theological formulations, the institutional and authoritarian structures of the church and its ministry, and the central role of the sacraments in the life of the church. This reformulation of the older churchly traditions was the direction taken by leading theologians in certain Protestant denominations. Charles Hodge was the architect of the Princeton theology in Presbyterian orthodoxy. The Oxford Movement through the writings of John Keble, John Henry Newman, and Edward B. Pusey influenced a rebirth of High-Church Anglicanism in America. Carl F.W. Walther restated Lutheran confessionalism in the Missouri Synod. The Mercersburg theology of John W. Nevin and Philip Schaff[3] reaffirmed traditional views of the church and sacraments in the German Reformed Church.

In light of the crisis in understanding the nature and mission of the church, other groups chose the path of restorationism, a return to the church in the New Testament. The Mormon Church, founded by Joseph Smith, claimed to have restored that church. Elias Smith, Abner Jones, and James O'Kelly led in restoration movements in America. This was also the direction taken by Barton W. Stone, leader of the "Christians" in Kentucky, and Walter Scott and the Campbells, who spearheaded the "Reformers" or Disciples. Their united efforts gave birth to a new religious movement on the American frontier, known as the Christian Church or Disciples of Christ.

The Church in Splendor, Without Spot or Wrinkle

The guiding principles for the movement initiated by

the Campbells and Scott were the restoration of the New Testament church and Christian union.[4] The restorationism of the Campbells and Scott reflected the influence of the eighteenth century Scottish Independents: Glas, Sandeman, and the Haldanes. In Scott's thinking, Alexander Campbell had restored the Ancient Order of the church, whereas it was his own specific achievement to have recovered the Ancient Gospel for the church. According to Scott and the Reformers, the restoration of the New Testament church (communal practices, worship, ordinances, and government) and its message of the Ancient Gospel was for the reunion of the fragmented church of the nineteenth century. Moreover, only the restoration of the New Testament church in its pristine purity could preserve the church in the face of the threats of Roman Catholicism and the multiplication of the Protestant sects.

There was an overall strategy in the mind of Scott and his associates in their movement for restoration. What was needed was a radical rethinking of the church in the light of its portrayal in the New Testament. The New Testament was the only guide to the church, its nature, its life and practices; it was perceived as a blueprint or organizational plan for the church in all of its details. The church was not to be constituted by creeds, confessions, or articles of faith, but solely by the New Testament.[5] Thus, the Ancient Order needed to be restored to the church of their day, and the Ancient Gospel was to be preached throughout the world for the conversion of sinners. Preaching of the Ancient Gospel would cause sectarianism to be overcome, and all of the churches would be united. Since sectarianism was viewed as a stumbling block in the way of the coming Kingdom of God (Isa. 57:14), its removal and the union of the churches would be a prelude to the long-awaited millennial age.

In his overall understanding of the church, Scott was in agreement with Thomas and Alexander Campbell that the church of Christ as described in the New Testament was one. The common bond uniting all of the churches was belief in the messiahship of Jesus Christ and a similarity in organizational structure, worship, and communal practices. Each local congregation was an independent, autonomous unit. The church as the body of Christ was not a collection of separate churches in the aggregate. In his organic conception of the church, Scott believed that each local congregation was a particular manifestation of the one universal church in the world.[6]

Scott's understanding of the church was based upon the fundamental conviction that Jesus of Nazareth is the Son of God and Messiah. He located the beginning of the church at the baptism of Jesus by John at the Jordan River, the descent of the Holy Spirit, and the declaration by God the Father that Jesus was his beloved Son in whom he was well-pleased (Matt. 3:16-17). This was the only direct revelation made by God to humanity; it was the primal act in the establishment of the church and was its constitutional basis.[7] As Jesus Christ was the foundation of the church, he formed the church by calling the disciples and bringing them into it. According to Scott's reading of the New Testament, the first person to be baptized by Jesus was Simon Peter. By this act, Peter was "the first stone laid on this well-tried rock."[8]

One of the most significant events in the beginning of the church, and a favorite text in Scott's preaching, was the confession of Jesus as the Christ by Simon Peter at Caesarea Philippi. This event was to impress upon the minds of the disciples that the messiahship of Jesus was the central truth of the Kingdom, the constitutional basis of the church, and that on this foundation Christ would build His church.[9] To Peter were given the keys to the Kingdom of heaven (Matt. 16:19), and by "keys" Scott meant the "principles of faith, repentance, and obedience in baptism, which open the Kingdom of God."[10] The church, which was founded on this truth and conviction regarding the messiahship of Jesus, was conceived as the Kingdom, and persons were born into it by water and the Spirit. Scott described the role of the church in the world:

> The church of God is an "imperium in imperio," a divine government in the midst of worldly governments, a moral kingdom in the midst of political ones; it is in the world, but "not of the world;" . . . When the Religion of Christ is contemplated and set forth under the figure of a kingdom, it is to be spoken of accordingly. Jesus is the king. Christians are the subjects. The whole globe is the territory. The New Testament contains its laws. Jerusalem is its capital. It began in the days of the Caesars. It will terminate only with eternity; and men are born into it in a manner agreeably to the will of God, that is, by "water and Spirit;" in a word, men are begotten to God by hearing and believing the gospel, and born to him by obeying it. But in all this the literal gospel is not changed; it still is believe, repent, and be baptized.[11]

In his understanding of the church, Scott divided the message it preaches and teaches into two fundamental divisions, the evangelical and ecclesiastical.[12] The church has a distinct message for the world and sinful humanity. The message for the world, the evangelical, consists of the proposition regarding the messiahship of Jesus Christ, which rests upon the scriptural evidences of miracles and prophecy fulfilled, and the six steps in the process of salvation. Although Scott's primary emphasis was on the evangelical division and the message of the gospel for the world, he wrote a number of articles in *The Evangelist* about the message for the church and the ordering of its life — the ecclesiastical division. He defined the church in these words:

> The church is an assemblage of Christ's disciples, associated on the principle of faith, derived from the Holy Scriptures; and therefore, such society ought to acknowledge no other book besides the Holy Scriptures, as the rule of its faith and morals, discipline, ordinances, manners, and customs.[13]

In his understanding of the ecclesiastical division of the church,[14] Scott's views were in agreement with those of Campbell concerning the Ancient Order. Both Scott and Campbell viewed the New Testament as the constitution that is to govern the life and affairs of the church.

Church Union: That They May All Be One

One of Walter Scott's principal concerns, as expressed in his periodicals and theological writings, was church union. In his approach to the question of the nature and character of church union, Scott conceived it in terms of the total history of the church and not simply as a necessity in light of the sectarianism on the American frontier in the nineteenth century. He viewed the history of the church as comprised of three eras from the time of Christ to the millennium: Primitive Christianity, the Apostasy, and the Reformation.[15] In America Christianity has appeared in three distinct forms: Roman Catholicism, the Lutheran Reformation, and the New Reformation of the nineteenth century with which Scott associated himself. In addressing the problem of church union, Scott's emphasis was on the principles that underlay the New Reformation and its central thrust. He identified three steps of development leading to church union in its full fruition: chaos (Roman Catholicism), analysis or resolution (Protestantism), and synthesis or reconstruction (the nineteenth century Reformation).[16]

The Vicar of Christ: Perpetuation of a Falsehood

The Christian Church had been brought into being in the age of Primitive Christianity but in time became fragmented. It was God's plan to recreate the church, but this could not be accomplished until the Apostolic Church had fallen into chaos. Roman Catholicism, which Scott equated with the historical development and ongoing life of the Apostolic Church for fifteen hundred years, was in a chaotic condition at the time of the Protestant Reformation. It was "a mass of the most discordant elements"[17] and was fundamentally in error.

In order to understand Scott's conception of Roman Catholicism, one must see his ideas in light of the broad anti-Catholic sentiment prevalent in America from the 1820's till the eve of the Civil War. The idea that Catholics represented a kind of spiritual despotism had been expressed earlier by Thomas Jefferson. The large number of Roman Catholic immigrants during the mid-nineteenth century occasioned an upsurge of American nativism and anti-Catholicism.[18] Increasingly Protestants viewed the Catholics as importing a foreign religion that was under the control of the pope in Rome. With the rapid growth of Catholicism, fears and doubts mounted about the future of American democracy. Lyman Beecher, Samuel F.B. Morse, Horace Bushnell, and other Protestant leaders feared that the large Catholic immigration was a plot by the pope and the Jesuits to control American religion and government. Nativistic anti-Catholic societies came into being. Numerous evangelical periodicals, books, and tracts gave increasingly more space to denouncing the Catholics. Much of this literature was lurid and salacious in detail and had a broad appeal to the populace. Suspicion and fear led to acts of violence as Catholic churches and convents were raided and burned.

Scott was extremely caustic in his views of Roman Catholicism and especially its status in America. He engaged in a scathing denunciation of the Catholic system of doctrine and church government. The particular object of his attack was the pope as the Vicar of Christ and the doctrine of papal infallibility.[19] From Scott's viewpoint the Catholics did not have the kind of union for which Christ had prayed. It was a forced unity and uniformity of doctrine that consolidated all spiritual authority in the person of the pope.[20] The

Catholic Church was wrong from its foundation and was constituted on the basis of "the lie" (*to pseudei*) mentioned in II Thess. 2:11.

> It is that a man, not God's Son, is the foundation of the Church. It is that the Church is built on Peter — not on Christ! The whole Catholic world is, as Scripture foretold and we behold, given up by God to believe this radical, this constitutional falsehood.[21]

Scott continued his attack on Catholicism and the pope:

> To make Peter the basis of the Church, and the Pope his successor, was to create a spiritual despotism. The Pope, as everyone knows, is . . . a despot in religion as the Czar is in the empire, and can, therefore, have no more sympathy with Protestantism, original Christianity, or republicanism, than the Emperor of Austria.[22]

In Scott's thinking there was no hope of effecting church union by way of Catholicism. The Catholics, or false church, would not be converted from the dogma of papal infallibility. The Papists, as Scott referred to them, and the Protestants in their present status were irreconcilable, because the Papists had set the church above the Scriptures and could not be reasoned with on the basis of scriptural authority. Ultimately, according to Scott, Catholicism would be destroyed in the ongoing processes of history as prophesied in Rev. 17:16.[23]

Scott's denunciation was not limited to the religious realm and his criticism of the Catholic Church's theological stance. It also extended to the question of the growth of Catholicism in the United States in the nineteenth century and what this could possibly mean for the nation. During the 1830's and 1840's he and many of the Disciples leaders became seriously concerned over the increase of the Catholic population. In 1841 Scott warned that the great influx of Jesuits and their activities in the country could well be the first step by Rome to overthrow the United States government.[24] A few years earlier he had urged legislative action banning further immigration of Catholics and the granting of citizenship to them. He stated his case in strong terms:

> If they cannot be at once a subject of the Pope, and a citizen of the United States, then let our courts of law, cease to extend to them that citizenship for which Protestants eminently bled and died under the great fathers of the Revolution, and if any law of prohibition be framed, let it run thus: "That no Catholic, or subject of the Pope of Rome, shall emigrate to the United States." We are no alarmists; but we pledge ourselves to prove, that every true Catholic is a subject of the Pope of Rome, and as such, is not entitled to citizenship of these States.[25]

For religious and political reasons Catholicism was corrupt, in chaos, and represented a threat to America and especially to Protestantism and the New Reformation. Hence, Scott and the Protestant leaders in America made no effort to converse with the Catholics on the question of church union.

Reforming a Corrupt Church: The Protestant Consciousness

Scott referred to the second stage in the recovery of the church as analysis or resolution. It was associated with the Reformation of the sixteenth century, especially with Luther and Calvin. Their labors and thought prepared the way for the Reformation of the nineteenth century. Scott summarized the work of Luther in his analysis of the Catholic Church on the eve of the Protestant Reformation:

> In the morning of the Lutheran reformation, therefore, the Catholic religion lay dark and heavily on the nations, a perfect chaos, ... Luther arose, and in Protestantism gave an analysis of our religion. He resolved it into its separate elements, took out of the Catholic chaos the parts of the watch, but could not put them up again in their original order, beauty, perfection, and simplicity.[26]

In his understanding of Protestantism, Scott was able to appreciate the positive accomplishments of the Reformation. In their respective analyses of Catholicism, Luther placed the church above the ministry, and Calvin placed the Bible above the church and the ministry.[27] As a result of their work there has developed what Scott called the "Protestant consciousness," consisting of four leading principles — the supremacy of the Scriptures, the subordination of the church to them, the subordination of the ministry to both, and the doctrine of justification by faith.[28] Giving a positive assessment to the work of the Protestant Reformers and what this has meant for the Christian faith, Scott wrote:

> We have before us all the great positive truths which, in the historical recovery of original Christianity, have been fixed as such in the consciousness of Protestants, and led to the glorious results of free inquiry, free discussion, and the other imperishable rights and liberties which form the heritage of the age.[29]

Even though the Reformation of the sixteenth century

was able to point to the errors in Roman Catholicism and offer valuable theological directions for the church, certain weaknesses pervaded the Protestant world and the various Protestant sects.[30] Scott advanced three principal criticisms of Protestantism in America. First, although the Scriptures were authoritative for the Protestants, they concentrated too much on correct doctrinal formulation to the neglect of Christian union. Scott, therefore, viewed Protestantism in America as the history of sects that were hostile to and warring with one another.[31] The partisanship and sectarian character of Protestantism was a major weakness. He saw sectarianism as pervasive on the American frontier and especially on the Western Reserve where he had begun his evangelistic activities. Scott's second criticism of the Protestant sects was directed toward their emphasis on creeds and theological systems.[32] These groups were guilty of placing in their creeds truths or articles of faith of a subordinate character, such as the doctrine of the Trinity. Because of this undue emphasis on certain articles in the creeds, Scott believed the creeds were basically divisive in nature.[33] The Protestant sects were pitted against one another, and the impact of the church on society was enervated. The third pervasive weakness Scott found in Protestantism was that in their creeds and preaching they failed to elevate the central element in the New Testament, namely, the truth that Jesus Christ is the Messiah and Son of God. On this point Scott noted:

> "Protestants believe in the Divinity of Christ." Granted; but that only as an element of the Trinity, not as the sole magnet of faith, intended for great practical purposes. In

some Confessions the Creed is eclipsed, mixed up with various other articles of belief, but not sufficiently illustrious above them. . . . In some, it is not even a published element at all. It is with most Protestant parties 'a' revelation, but not, as in Scripture, by way of eminence, 'the' revelation.[34]

Scott's view was that the Protestant groups were not following the true order of the New Testament and preaching the faith as delivered by Christ to His apostles. Not only did they not give due consideration to the divinity of Christ and His messiahship, but they did not rightly understand the New Testament plan of salvation and the correct order in which it was to be preached. In Scott's formulation the individual was to have faith, repent, and be baptized. Following these God would remit one's sins, give the Holy Spirit, and promise eternal life to the believer.[35]

The Church Purified and Restored: A Plan of Union

The third stage of development in the recovery of the church, synthesis or reconstruction, was the work of the Reformation of the nineteenth century. Scott believed that the Protestant churches of his day needed to be reconstructed, thereby preparing the way for Christian union.[36] In order to understand the central thrust of the New Reformation and its plea for Christian union, one must see it in relation to other efforts for union in the early and mid-nineteenth century. By doing this, one is able to see more clearly the distinctiveness and radical nature of the New Reformation and their proposals.

Samuel S. Schmucker, a Lutheran, in his *Fraternal Appeal to the American Churches*,[37] in 1838, urged the churches to abandon their party names and unite to form the Apostolic Protestant Church. Schmucker's appeal for unity was based on a common confession of faith, consisting of twelve articles derived from the creeds of several churches and expressing the fundamental truths of the Christian faith. The churches should practice intercommunion and have an interchangeable ministry. Schmucker's plan allowed the denominations to keep their respective organizational structures, use their historic forms of worship, and utilize their own creeds if they desired, provided they accept the twelve articles of the Apostolic Protestant Church. If his plan had been accepted, the result would have been a federation of churches rather than a united church.[38]

Within the Protestant Episcopal Church, proposals to unite the churches were put forth by Thomas Hubbard Vail and William Reed Huntington. One of the more celebrated endeavors for union was by William A. Muhlenberg, who inaugurated the Memorial Movement[39] in 1853 in an effort to make the Protestant Episcopal church an instrument for effecting Christian union in America. His plan for union was based on extending Episcopal ordination and a measure of pastoral oversight to sincere ministers of other denominations, provided they would abide by certain liturgical, administrative, and doctrinal requirements of the church.

Nineteenth century Protestantism witnessed the formation of other movements that sought to achieve a type of unity in action. Basic to many of these was the idea that theological and ecclesiastical differences could be ignored or forgotten, and unity could be achieved by Christian people through benevolent activity. In this "benevolent empire" individuals, but not established denominations, cooperated in various educational, missionary, and reform endeavors. Included in these enterprises were Methodists, Reformed, Congregationalists, Low Church Episcopalians, Baptists, and Presbyterians. These persons believed that all Christians were one; by working together a spirit of unity could be achieved. Essentially, these endeavors were pragmatic in their thrust and represented not a reconciling but a concealing of theological issues through activism. Among these were the American Bible Society, the American Home Missionary Society, the American Tract Society, the American Sunday School Union, and the Evangelical Alliance.[40]

Numerous other endeavors for union and cooperation among the churches appeared on the horizon in nineteenth century America. The Plan of Union (1801) and the Accommodation Plan (1808) were developed by the Presbyterians and Congregationalists in the work of missions and evangelism on the frontier. The Evangelical Church of the Prussian Union was formed in 1817 by Frederick William III in Germany. Inspired by this union, many of the German Reformed and Lutherans in Pennsylvania engaged in cooperative efforts in worship and evangelism and looked forward to a union. Other voices were heard advocating church union, prominent among whom were Philip Schaff and John Williamson Nevin at the German Reformed seminary in Mercersburg, Pennsylvania.

Over against these various attempts by Lutherans, Episcopalians, and others to establish a basis for Christian union, Scott and the Reformers with whom he was associated put forth their plan. They advocated a restoration of Primitive Christianity in both its structural form and theological content by returning to the New Testament. Regarding the New Testament and the union of Christians, Scott's primary emphasis was on restoring to the church the Creed, by which he meant the proposition that Jesus Christ is the Messiah and Son of God.[41] The messiahship of Jesus Christ was not only the basis of the church and salvation, but it was also conceived as the principle of Christian union. This was the synthesis and reconstruction needed by the church in the nineteenth century. If the Protestant sects of the day would accept the Creed and the principles derived from it, namely, the six steps in the plan of salvation, Christian union would become a reality.[42] Thus, the union which Scott called for did not entail subscribing to creedal statements or having doctrinal uniformity.[43] It meant accepting the truths of Primitive Christianity as contained in the New Testament. He summed up his overall conception of the nature of Christian union:

> The Scriptures discriminate, I believe, between the following matters:
> 1. The basis of union.
> 2. The bond of peace; and
> 3. The bond of perfection.
> The first of these is the Messiahship; the second is the solemn consideration that there is but one Christian body or Church — one spirit, one hope, one Lord, one faith, one baptism, and one God and Father to all the

brethren. The third is love. Love is the bond of perfection; our moral nature is perfected by love. . . . It is one thing, therefore, to sit down as a Church on the Messiahship; it is a second to preserve the peace when sitting there; and it is a third matter in this union and peace to perfect ourselves in love. The three expressions above refer severally to constitutional union, the general peace, and to personal perfection.[44]

Scott believed that there was hope for Christian union by way of Protestantism and the Protestant sects. The work of Luther and Calvin in restoring the Scriptures to a position of authority was especially significant. Scott and the nineteenth century Reformers accepted all of their positive achievements as expressed in the "Protestant consciousness." Protestantism, however, was conceived by Scott as a stepping stone from chaos to synthesis; it was provisional and in a state of transition.[45] The final stage in the recovery of the church was being accomplished by the Reformers of the nineteenth century in their reconstruction of the church, thereby overcoming the failings and shortcomings of Protestantism. The Protestant sects would dissolve in the light of the preaching of the true message of the New Testament by the Reformers, and union would be realized. Scott stated what would take place:

As Moses' rod ate up the rods of the magicians, the true Creed will destroy all others, and the true principles of union consume all those of mere party origin. Reformers, having hitherto failed to select and appreciate the constitutional truth of the Christian system, their labors became schismatic, and they themselves the founders of sects. The aims and destinies of the holders of the true faith are higher. Their mission is Union — the annihilation of sects and parties, and the recovery of the church. . . .

That will be the Creed, which, being proved true, proves all things else in the Gospel true; and that the church, which, being founded on the true Creed, shall bind in union, communion, and co-operation, all the individual assemblies of which she is composed.[46]

Scott was not advocating an organic union of all Protestants or a merger to form one large church. His conception was that the churches of his day have a union such as existed among the early Christians living in the same city or district.[47] He described the kind of union he found in the Apostolic Church:

These Churches being everywhere "constitutionally" the same . . . the members passed from one organization to another by letters of introduction and commendation, and when Churches co-operated it was by districts, and not by parties, as in Protestantism, or by the Pope, as in Romanism. . . . This was a safe sort of union, because it secured the co-operation of the Churches without endangering their liberties by the centralization of spiritual power in any individual. It was conservative both of the liberty and the strength of the Churches. It was God's plan of union.[48]

This kind of union as a relationship among the churches and their members could become an actuality in the nineteenth century, according to Scott. The true Creed could bind all of the churches in a spirit of unity, cooperation, and commonality of belief. The churches would have in reality a common, interchangeable membership, and sectarian barriers would no longer exist.[49] In order to bring about the kind of Christian union he envisioned, Scott issued a plea for a great convocation among the Protestants to discuss its possibility. Regarding this assemblage, Scott suggested the following purpose:

> The times call for a Union Society, that by its preaching, teaching, printing, and publications, shall change the spirit of the age from schism to Union. All the friends of evangelical Christianity are loudly called on by the times, by the prevalence of infidelity, and the increase of the Papacy to surrender every prejudice of the faith; popularity to principle; party policy to the general interests of the Church of God; and every other inferior consideration to the great duty of Union and the conversion of mankind.[50]

They Shall Reign With Him A Thousand Years

Along with the restoration of New Testament Christianity and the reunion of the churches, the approaching millennium was another of the central concerns of Scott and the Reformers. The notion that the thousand year period when Christ would reign (Rev. 20:1-6) was near at hand was widespread from the mid-1820's throughout the antebellum period. The conviction of the nearness of the millennium and what it would mean for all mankind was very prominent in Scott's early writing and preaching. In 1826 he wrote two articles, "On the Millennium," in *The Christian Baptist*; in the first he declared:

> Mankind is certainly moving in the horizon of some great and eventful change, into the centre of which all society must inevitably and speedily be carried. The world is in strange commotion; expectation is all aroused — anticipation of something good, splendid, and unknown, is becoming undoubting and impatient,

even to painfulness; and the time is at hand when a plenteous harvest of toil and talent must be reaped from all orders of society, that many may run to and fro, and knowledge be increased. . . .
. . . This is the "millennial" or "evangelical" age of the world; during which the human race will enjoy great happiness.[51]

In 1827 he drew up a prospectus for a monthly paper to be called "The Millennial Herald," although he did not commence its publication. In his address to the Mahoning Baptist Association in 1828, Scott was concerned principally with the subject of the millennium.[52]

In Scott's thinking, there was a sequence of events that would follow the recovery and preaching of the Ancient Order and the Ancient Gospel: the spread of the gospel, the conversion of sinners, the dissolution of sectarianism, the reunion of the churches, and the transformation of society. These events would precede and usher in the millennial age. A sense of urgency and excitement was shared by Scott and his associates in the New Reformation. They believed that they were part of a great drama and active participants in the work of realizing the Kingdom of God.[53] They were on the threshold of an event that would be the culmination of human progress, the fulfillment of the promises of God, and the result of God's providential guidance. It was this expectation of the imminent millennium that gave Scott's preaching of the Ancient Gospel such power and accounted in great measure for his phenomenal success on the Western Reserve during the years 1827-1830 and in the succeeding years.[54]

Beginning around 1830 a new wave of millennial

excitement swept through the American frontier with great fervor. Some of the most prominent Protestant ministers of the day became intensely interested in the subject of the millennium and its nearness. The scriptural prophecies regarding the Second Coming of Christ were studied carefully. Much of this excitement centered around William Miller (1782-1849),[55] a New England farmer who began around 1831 to preach the nearness of the end. The followers of Miller, called "Millerites" or "Adventists," spread their message over the whole northeastern part of the United States and New England. Between 1840-1844, the movement had achieved epidemic proportions and was nationwide in scope. Essentially, Miller's idea was that Christ would soon appear physically and inaugurate the one thousand year reign. A prominent feature of his premillennialism was a prediction as to the time when Christ would come. Miller's studies of the scriptural prophecies and chronological calculations pointed to 1843 and later to 1844 as the dates of the Advent.

This premillennial excitement generated by Miller and others was shared by Scott and Barton W. Stone from the early 1830's until the mid-1840's.[56] During this time Scott's periodical, *The Evangelist*, was filled with premillennial speculation. From June 1834 to May 1835 he wrote a series of eight articles entitled "The Second Coming of Christ: The Cloud," in which he interpreted the scriptural passages regarding the Advent and the attendant circumstances in a literal manner. Scott was very specific as to the descent of Christ from heaven on a cloud, accompanied by the holy angels. When Christ comes He will be seated on a throne or chariot. His coming will be unexpected and sudden as a flash of lightning and will inaugurate the millennium.[57] During these years Scott was greatly excited over the idea of the Second Coming of Christ, but he did not share the view of the Millerites regarding the precise time when Christ would appear. He did not believe one could have a fixed chronology concerning the time of the Advent as was being urged by Miller and his followers.[58]

In the mid-1840's Scott changed his viewpoint on the thousand year reign of Christ from premillennialism to postmillennialism. This change was due principally to the failure of the Millerite philosophy in 1844 and to the influence of Alexander Campbell, who held a postmillennial viewpoint throughout this period.[59] Scott's later ideas were presented most comprehensively in *The Messiahship* under the rubric, "Political Christianity,"[60] In his treatment of the millennium, Scott interpreted the biblical symbols and prophetic passages, not from the viewpoint of premillennialism, but from the perspective of Enlightenment optimism and postmillennialism. Especially important for him was Isa. 65:17: "For behold, I create new heavens and a new earth." In his discussion of the coming millennium, the ideas of progress and Manifest Destiny[61] were very prominent.

Although the idea of Manifest Destiny was expressed in different conceptual forms, the fundamental thought was that the Anglo-Saxons were God's chosen people in America to bring blessings to all humanity. The concept of Manifest Destiny in America extended back to the colonial days. It was prominent in the Puritan sense of divine mission. As servants of God their task was to build the Kingdom of God, a society controlled by the regenerated and regulated by God's will as revealed in Scripture. In the nineteenth century many of the Protestant church leaders adhered to the Manifest Destiny vision. They believed that their mission was to expand democratic government and Christian civilization across the American continent and then throughout the world. Through human progress (Enlightenment optimism) and guided by the providence of God, an age of peace and prosperity would ultimately be realized in America. A great empire of righteousness and liberty would be built in America and would spread to all nations of the world. This optimistic, utopian philosophy was pervasive throughout the nineteenth century in America and underlay much of the Disciples thinking. This conviction regarding the destiny of America was in Scott's thinking inextricably connected with a postmillennial philosophy of history. In his development of "Political Christianity," the coming millennium became basically a Protestant form of Manifest Destiny and the American dream interpreted prophetically.

According to his understanding of the coming millennium, there would be the "new heavens and a new earth" as prophesied in Isa. 65:17. By these symbols Scott meant "a new government and a new people." In the millennial age, the old idolatrous governments would be destroyed, and new governments and a new civilization would appear.[62] In this new society to come Christianity would be glorified as the true religion, and the church of Jesus Christ would rejoice. In the millennial age governments would continue to exist, although they would be headed by persons of a different character than the tyrannical governments of the present time.

The millennium would be a time when there would be a double rule: an inner and an outer government. The inner government, a spiritual one, would be in the hands of Christ through His church. This inner government of Christ, the Kingdom of God or the church, had already been established for eighteen hundred years and was exercising its rule at the present time. The outer political government, which would be in the hands of God's saints, was identified with the type of government in the United States, because this was Christ's nation.[63] In the millennial age, with the new government and new people (new heavens and new earth), the rule of the Messiah would be complete. Referring to the prophecy of Daniel, Scott wrote:

> All the types, then, pointed to the time when the inner government would go into the hands of Christ, and all the symbols to the time when the outer should go into the hands of Christians, and the world both politically and spiritually the Lord's.[64]

As Scott envisioned the coming millennium, America was to have a decisive role. The United States was the first of the Messianic nations, "the sum of all the progress that has been made on this continent since its discovery by Columbus."[65] In conceiving America as the first of the Messianic nations, he was not implying that the millennium had already been actualized here. The American Revolution in effect meant the creation of a new government and a new society, a vital step in the ongoing progress of humanity toward the coming Golden Age (the millennium). Thus, in Scott's thinking religious liberty and democratic government belonged together in America, as he stated clearly:

> In the United States the two forms of liberty, the political
> and the religious, are, it is confessed, well-defined, and,
> as we trust, permanently established. The internal and
> external, the civil and religious, the government of
> Caesar and the government of God, have each found its
> proper basis in our country — the one in the Bible, the
> other in the general constitution, and both in the public
> consciousness. Thus the two great interests intended to
> conserve and defend both soul and body are enjoyed
> here in perfection.[66]

Scott gave other reasons why the United States was a
Messianic nation:

> It is now for the Reader to judge and decide for himself
> whether there are in the elements of the Revolution of
> 1776 unmistakable proofs that the Republic of the
> United States is a historical and political verification of
> the unerring prediction of prophecy touching "a new
> government" and "a new people." If he decides in the
> affirmative, he will then see, with the writer, that the
> long-looked for age, popularly styled "The Millennium,"
> must belong to the history of human progress, and be of
> gradual introduction. He will see that it is not an age to
> drop down from heaven, but a period of light, religion
> and enjoyment to arise out of the natural and gradual
> progress of society. Revolution must succeed revolution
> in all lands, till the rights and liberties of humanity are
> understood and restored to all nations. . . . it remains for
> the reader to decide whether the United States is not one
> of the new Messianic governments predicted by the
> prophets; and whether there is not far more of reason
> than romance in our views of the matter.[67]

Scott also viewed Great Britain as a Messianic nation.
Our goal as Messianic nations was to spread the gospel
to all nations of the world and thereby be instrumental

in the realization of the millennium. When the Christian gospel was preached, nations would change through revolution. They would become democratic nations where the Christian faith, liberty, and justice for all prevailed. Through the slow process of human achievement and progress, guided by the providence of God, the millennium would come, and the ancient prophecies of "new heavens and a new earth" would be fulfilled. Scott expressed his Christian philosophy of the destiny of the United States and Great Britain:

> Among the Christian governments of the old world . . . none unfurls a broader and more glorious banner than Great Britain. . . .
> But admitting the greatness and glory of the English Ensign, it is perhaps only in America, in the United States, that we see the banner of human rights floating highest, and its billowy foldings made most resplendent by the light of the Sun of Righteousness. In Great Britain and the United States we have before us, one in the new and one in the old world, the most illustrious proofs that the Messiah who was to come is come, and that the better order of things indicated in the prophets is inaugurated in these two governments at least.[66]

God Shed His Grace On Thee

Because of his optimistic view of the destiny of the American nation and his conception of human progress towards the coming millennial age, Scott loved his country and its institutions with a deep passion. Here in the United States the human mind was unlimited in its growth, development, and possibilities; it had a freer scope than it had ever enjoyed in history. In America the

Christian churches had the opportunity to spread the gospel and demonstrate the superiority of Christianity as the true religion. Even though Scott had a deep commitment to the Christian faith and a love for the nation, there was in his thinking a separation of church and state. There should be no entanglements or alliances between the churches and the United States Government, no establishment of religion by law, such as was characteristic of some states in the Colonial Era and immediately following the American Revolution.[69]

Scott wrote a tract on the subject of patriotism,[70] in which he expressed the view that being a patriot is thoroughly consistent with being a Christian. One can in all integrity be a Christian patriot, according to Scott, patriotism being defined as "the love of country, the love of our fellow-citizens in particular."[71] His argument in defense of patriotism was based on the Scriptures. Although God loves all persons with benevolence, he has a special love for the believers. Christ Himself loved in particular the Jews, His kinsmen and lived especially for them. For these reasons Christianity does teach patriotism, which is a superior regard for one's countrymen.[72] Christian patriotism meant for Scott that one should hold one's nation in the highest esteem and desire that society be filled with persons of a Christian character who have faith in God and in Jesus Christ; this will insure stability to the social order and to political institutions.[73] All of the resources of the nation, then, should be directed toward the formation of Christian virtues in the lives of its citizens. Concerning the character and role of the Christian patriot, Scott wrote:

He is the Christian patriot who, having arrayed himself
with the gifts and graces of the divine nature, ... does
afterward labor to induce the same form of divine
nature upon all his countrymen, and by finished life and
lovely perfection swell the note of his country's
applause among foreign nations and before God the
supreme ruler of the world. Yes, he is the true patriot,
and all other forms of patriotism are bastard and illegiti-
mate and will at last fail to inherit the commendation of
God.[74]

Let My People Go!

Walter Scott was deeply concerned for and expressed
himself on the major political and social issues of the
day. In his writings and preaching he voiced his opinion
on such matters as temperance, labor problems, immigration, pacifism, and war. One of the most pressing
and poignant issues in early and mid-nineteenth century America, over which deep passions were generated, was the slavery question.[75]

Slavery had been one of the most deeply entrenched
institutions of society, extending back to the early days
of settlement in America. Slaveholders defended it,
humanitarians attacked it. The antislavery advocates
fervently believed in the freedom of all people in the
sight of God. For a nation conceived in liberty and des-
tined to be a beacon of light to the world, slavery was a
blight and an ugly blot. Others, especially the Southern
plantation owners and businessmen, viewed slavery as
an institution vitally necessary for their economy and
way of life. God had provided it, and it was sanctioned
by Scripture. Certain northern businessmen, also, feared

that there would be a loss of revenue for them if slavery were abolished.

It was inevitable that tensions would mount as both sides became more deeply entrenched in their convictions. Slavery became the subject of national debates. Bitter conflicts and heated passions developed over federalism versus States' rights, admitting new states to the Union, colonization of the Negroes, and abolition. Churches entered the arena of debate with ardor and spiritual convictions; pronouncements were made by the churches on both sides of the question.

Essays condemning slavery poured forth from the presses. The American Colonization Society endeavored to return the Negroes to their native shores of Africa. Abolition societies appeared. William Lloyd Garrison, an ardent champion of abolition, published the first edition of "The Liberator" on January 1, 1831. He passionately urged the abrupt termination of slavery and granting full rights to the Negroes. More moderate anti-slavery voices were heard advocating a gradual emancipation of the slaves.

In the 1850's the slavery question continued to generate heated passions with unabated intensity. The hearts of all were deeply touched, both with pathos and anger, with the publication of Harriet Beecher Stowe's *Uncle Tom's Cabin* in 1852. One and a half million copies were sold in five years. Simon Lagree soon became a symbol of cruelty to the slaves in the minds of the Northerners; the book was anathema in the South. The Kansas-Nebraska bill, sponsored by Stephen A. Douglas in 1854, permitted these territories the right of self-determination in the matter of slavery. Subsequent fighting continued in "bleeding Kansas" between the proponents of slavery and the forces opposing it. The famous Dred Scott decision issued by the Supreme Court in 1857 ruled that a Negro slave who was held by his master in a free state was not thereby a free person. In 1859 John Brown, the abolitionist, led an attack on the U.S. arsenal at Harpers Ferry in an effort to free the slaves in Maryland and Virginia. He was hanged on December 2, 1859, but as his body lay mouldering in the grave his spirit lived on as this action shook both the North and South. Thus, as the decade of the 1850's drew to a close a national crisis was impending, and dark clouds hung over the land.

Walter Scott, who lived through these troubled times and witnessed this train of events, was basically a Northern moderate who believed in emancipation but not an immediate or radical abolition. During the early years of their reform movement, he was in accord with Alexander Campbell and Barton W. Stone in advocating a gradual emancipation and colonization of the slaves. For the remainder of his life, Scott was a critic of the institution of slavery. Baxter wrote of him:

> He inclined to the views of the colonizationists, rather than those of the abolitionists, as the former proposed to return the emancipated blacks to their own country, while the latter demanded their instant and absolute liberation, without proposing any means, in his view, by which both master and slave might be able to bear the change with the least injury.[76]

Scott's views on the slavery question were expressed most clearly in his editorial exchange with Nathaniel Field, a staunch abolitionist in Jeffersonville, Indiana.

This ongoing exchange appeared in *The Evangelist* in 1834-1835.[77] Field, along with William Lloyd Garrison and others, advocated an immediate emancipation of the slaves and challenged Scott to adopt their position. For Field, an antislavery sentiment could only mean immediate abolition. If one was not an abolitionist, one was proslavery; there was no room for a middle ground such as was implied in gradual emancipation or colonization. Field charged that if Scott was not an abolitionist, he was an apologist for the institution of slavery and connected slavery with the principles of the gospel. He argued further that his own church at Jeffersonville, Indiana, and the Silver Creed Association had resolved not to have communion or break bread with slaveholders, nor even consider those who owned slaves to be Christians. Since slavery was a "citadel of the devil,"[78] its continuation was anathema and decidedly anti-Christian. According to Field, the leaders of the New Reformation and advocates of the Ancient Gospel should immediately disavow slavery and adopt the position of the abolitionists. Their movement for reform would be of no avail if it sanctioned slavery in any form.

In his response to Field, Scott countered that no church, in particular the church at Jeffersonville, could legislate on the slavery question or state categorically what the Christian position was. Scott believed that all religious questions should be dealt with in light of the Scriptures. On examining the Scriptures, he noted that slavery existed even before they were written. The early Christians held slaves and were not condemned for it by the apostles, as is seen in Paul's letter to Philemon.

Therefore, the Scriptures did not speak against slavery, nor did slavery derive its authority from the Scriptures. Slavery, then, was not a religious issue, and churches could not legislate regarding it. Scott noted that even in his day many people who were slaveholders were good Christian people and kind masters to their slaves. Even if Christians were to free their slaves the national problem would remain unsolved, since Christians were only a small portion of the total population of the country. In his moderate position on the slavery question, one can see Scott's underlying view of the separation of church and state.

Scott stressed repeatedly in his response to Field that he was not an advocate of slavery. He opposed both the commencement and continued existence of slavery. Even though it was a political evil and could not be condoned, Scott could not align himself with the abolitionists. Immediate manumission, such as was being urged by Field and others, left unsettled the question of what to do with the emancipated slaves. It further ignored the social and economic implications for the Southerners, whose livelihoods and businesses were dependent on the institution of slavery. Scott argued that the matter of the vested interests of the slaveholders should be taken into consideration.

Along with the great minds of the day, both in the religious and political realms, Scott admitted perplexity on the question of manumission and how it could be effected. He did see some possible courses of action that could be taken through political means. Since slavery was a political matter, it should be resolved by the individual states and the Federal Government. At the level of the slave states, the matter could be settled through the process of voting and majority rule. The Federal Government and the governments of the free states who desired emancipation should make appropriations of money that would compensate for the financial losses to the slaveholders. In Scott's thinking this was a reasonable means of emancipation; it would be just for those who owned slaves and also for the well-being of the freed slaves.

A House Divided Against Itself

As tensions over the slavery issue and States' rights mounted, the Northern and Southern states polarized. It was becoming increasingly clear that the clouds of war were gathering and that the nation would be plunged into civil conflict. During the fall of 1860 following the election of Abraham Lincoln to the presidency, Scott wrote his essay, "Crisis,"[79] which he addressed to thousands of his friends in the North and South. In the essay Scott attempted to turn the tide of secession and the imminent Civil War by making an earnest appeal for the preservation of the Union. He was a true patriot, loved his country with a deep passion, and did not wish to remain silent or to be neutral in the midst of this national crisis. He assessed the gravity of the situation facing the nation and wrote:

> Fraternal ties are being sundered, and sundered, I fear, forever. The Northern and Southern sections of our illustrious Republic, hitherto nurtured, like twin sisters, at the breasts of the same "magna mater virum," pur-

pose to discard the fraternal relations, and, as distinct nations, stand in the future to each other in the relations of peace or war, blood or gain. Some good-natured but not far-seeing men imagine that our Federal difficulties will disappear as certainly and suddenly as they were suddenly and unexpectedly developed. God grant they may; but brothers' quarrels are not lovers' quarrels, and it requires but little logic to foresee that, unless the black cloud that at present overhangs the great Republic is speedily buried in the deep bosom of the ocean, it will finally rain down war, bloodshed, and death on these hitherto peaceful and delightful lands.[80]

The core of Scott's argument for preservation of the Union was based on an analogy between the solar system and the Federal Government.[81] In both cases, according to him, an organic or systematic union is involved. The planets in the solar system are not a chaotic mass but were formed with a relationship to the sun as the vital center; secession in the solar system is totally unknown. By the same token the Federal Government comprised of the individual states is an organic union possessing stability, power, and permanence. A stable government cannot exist with isolated parts; therefore, secession is contrary to the nature of government. Speaking specifically of the issues at hand, Scott wrote:

Admit secession to be a law or right, the confederation is at once transfigured into a simple aggregation, and would then more fitly be called the "Disunited States," . . . I refer that the States being organic, a body politic, a confederation, a constitutional order of things, no single member can more legitimately divorce itself from the central government than can the central government legitimately divorce itself from the single State.[82]

Scott viewed the Federal Government as an instrument of human progress, "the rarest and most perfect piece of political workmanship ever framed by man." It is the hope for the spread of liberty and the blessings of Christianity to the other nations of the world. Secession will tear asunder the Federal Government and halt human progress. Since secession does not exist in the heavens, it must not be accepted by the people of our land regarding the government. Even though the government like all human institutions has imperfections, its unity, harmony, and integrity must be maintained. No state can secede from the Union without causing irreparable damage to itself and the other states.[83] Scott concluded his argument and plea for preservation of the Union:

> The government, therefore, that will not with all its "force," in defiance of all obstacles, put down anarchy and the doctrine that leads to it, ought itself to be put down, as men are more ready to follow a bad example than attend to a good precept. If this course is not pursued with personages working treason, others will imitate their insurrectionary precedent, till the infection of revolt spreading far and wide among the people, our Union will be dissolved and the United States Government perish in the whirlpool of bloody revolution. With this view of things, it would be impossible for me to admit the legitimacy of "secession," unless I could also admit that the United States Constitution contemplated its own future destruction and provided for it, which is absurd.[84]

Scott was deeply affected and grieved by the events of the day, the approaching Civil War, and the disruption of the unity of the nation. He wished to see the conflict resolved without bloodshed; union meant peace and secession meant war. Not only was this sentiment reflected in the "Crisis" essay but also in letters to his son in the last years of his life.[85] As late as 1859 he had published *The Messiahship*, in which he expressed an optimistic view of the destiny of America and progress toward the coming millennium. With the inevitability of secession and the Civil War, Scott's hopes for a bright future for his country, his vision of its destiny and divine mission as a Messianic nation, and his confidence in the progress of humanity were threatened. Baxter assessed the significance of the state of the nation for Scott:

> He now realized that there was no hope of a peaceful adjustment, and that the land of which he was proud to be a citizen, which had been a light to other lands was about to undergo a dark and bloody eclipse; this increased his sorrow and filled him with the most painful forebodings, for in the madness that ruled the hour he saw nothing but disaster and ruin, and feared that, in the storm of the impeding fraternal strife, the ship of state would be wrecked and the best hopes of humanity go down.[86]

Walter Scott died with broken dreams and in despair over the fate of the nation, and this also affected his religious beliefs. We have seen that his ideas of the progress of the church, the preaching of the Ancient Gospel, and his plan for Christian union were set within the context of Enlightenment optimism, human progress, and the grand destiny of America as a Messianic nation. Although Scott did not say specifically, one may surmise that with the approaching Civil War and the tearing asunder of the bonds of national unity, he was in dismay over the future of the New Reformation, the prospects for Christian union, and the progress of the church towards the millennial age.

Even though his life ended in sadness, history would show that his efforts were not in vain. He had labored long and faithfully to bring into being a new religious movement of which he was a formative figure. This movement did survive the fiery ordeal of civil conflict and has grown in strength since that time. All who stand in this tradition will continue to look upon Walter Scott as one of its pioneer spirits.

Footnotes

1. See Robert Baird, *Religion in America*, A Critical Abridgement with Introduction by Henry Warner Bowden (New York: Harper, 1970). This work of Baird, published in 1843, was the first panoramic history of the church in America and was the standard text used by subsequent church historians. For Baird, American Protestantism was principally the story of evangelical revivalism and voluntarism.

2. See H. Shelton Smith, Robert T. Handy, and Lefferts A. Loetscher, *American Christianity: An Historical Interpretation with Representative Documents*, II, 1820-1960 (New York: Scribner, 1963): 10-19, for a fuller discussion of the scope of the voluntary benevolent societies and the strength they received from revivalism.

3. Philip Schaff, *The Principles of Protestantism* trans. John W. Nevin, 1845, Bard Thompson and George H. Bricker, eds., Lancaster Series on the Mercersburg Theology, vol. 1 (Philadelphia: United Church Press, 1964), stated the principal ideas of the Mercersburg theology in a series of 112 theses.

4. Scott, "Address: given before the American Christian Missionary Society," pp. 30-31. In discussing the question of unity, Scott used the terms church union and Christian union interchangeably. His usage of terms usually depended on the context in which he was speaking or writing; more often, however, he referred to Christian union.

5. It was the contention of Scott and Campbell, in line with their orientation in Enlightenment rationalism, that one needed to return

to the Golden Age in the past. The New Testament church in the apostolic period was viewed as the Golden Age, during which time the church existed in a pure, uncorrupted state. Roman Catholicism had not yet led the church astray. Correct doctrine was still taught; the churches were constituted along the same lines; and they existed in a harmonious relationship with one another.

6. Scott, *The Messiahship*, p. 40. Here he was expressing the principal ideas that Thomas Campbell had enunciated concerning the oneness and universality of the church: "The Church of Christ upon earth is essentially, intentionally, and constitutionally one, consisting of all those in every place that profess their faith in Christ and obedience to Him in all things according to the scriptures, and that manifest the same by their tempers and conduct, and of none else, as none else can be truly and properly called Christians." (Thomas Campbell, *Declaration and Address*, p. 15).

The *Declaration and Address* was a manifesto for Christian union through restoration. Campbell was not describing the church in its fragmented state as it existed in the nineteenth century. The one universal church was the church as portrayed in the New Testament; it was also his idea of what the church of his day should and could be. His assumption was that the New Testament church was united in its faith, worship, and ordering; what was practiced in one church was practiced universally in the Early Church. All denominations could unite on the basis of an exact conformity to the New Testament regarding faith, worship, ordinances, and organizational patterns. Only what was specifically commanded in the New Testament could be normative for the restored church in the nineteenth century.

7. Scott, *A Discourse on the Holy Spirit*, pp. 8-9; and Scott, *The Gospel Restored*, pp. 143, 532-533.

8. Scott, *A Discourse on the Holy Spirit*, p. 9.

9. Scott, *The Gospel Restored*, pp. 140-141; and Scott, *The Messiahship*, pp. 244-245. Especially important for Scott were Matt. 3:13-17; 16:13-20; and Acts 2:38.

10. Scott, *To Themelion*, p. 27.

11. Scott, *The Gospel Restored*, pp. 199-200.

12. Scott, "Organization, No. 1." *The Evangelist* 10 (December 1842): 265.

13. Scott, "On Church Character, No. 1," *The Evangelist* 2 (August 1833): 145.

14. See Vernon Lee Fishback, "Some Influences of the Idea of the Messiahship in Walter Scott's Program of Church Life as Reflected in His Writings" (B.D. thesis, Butler University, 1949), pp. 43-87, for a discussion of Scott's understanding of the ecclesiastical division

and the New Testament program of church life as expressed in his periodicals and other theological writings. Fishback discusses various categories of church life, such as the government of the church, (the ministry, elders, evangelists, and deacons), worship (preaching, teaching, praying, singing, and scriptural reading), the ordinances (baptism and the Lord's Supper), discipline (private and public offenses), and New Testament manners and customs (hospitality, the holy kiss, handshakes, embraces, and foot washing).

15. *The Evangelist* 1 (January 1832): 19.

16. Scott, "Address," pp. 30-31.

17. Ibid., p. 31.

18. A fuller discussion of nativism and anti-Catholicism in America may be found in Ahlstrom, *A Religious History of the American People*, pp. 555-568.

19. Scott, *The Messiahship*, pp. 118-141. Scott used the words "papal infallibility," although this dogma was not declared officially until the Vatican Council of 1869-1870.

20. Scott, *To Themelion*, p. 42.

21. Ibid., p. 118.

22. Ibid., pp. 120-121.

23. Ibid., pp. 100, 121.

24. Scott, "The Romish Church Since the Reformation," *The Evangelist* 9 (May 1841): 101.

25. Scott, "Catholicism," *The Evangelist* 4 (December 1835): 280.

26. Scott, "Address," p. 31.

27. Scott, *The Messiahship*, pp. 275-276, 290.

28. Ibid., pp. 290-291.

29. Ibid., p. 290.

30. Scott, *To Themelion*, p. 101, viewed all of the Protestant denominations as "sects." In his thinking the principal Protestant sects were the Episcopalians, Methodists, Presbyterians, Lutherans, Baptists, and Independents.

31. Scott, "Address," pp. 31-32.

32. Scott, *He Nekrosis*, pp. 30-46, mentioned certain contemporary theological systems he opposed: Arminianism, Calvinism, Roman Catholicism, Mormonism and Universalism. He was critical of all creedal formulations, especially the Philadelphia Confession of Faith (Baptists) and the Westminster Confession of Faith (Presbyterians).

33. Scott, *To Themelion*, p. 40. Scott's view of creeds, for example, was opposite to that of the strict Lutheran confessionalism of Carl F.W. Walther, who urged that Christians were committed to the doctrines expressed in the ecumenical creeds of the church and the historic confessions of Lutheranism.

34. Ibid., p. 37. Scott acknowledged that all Protestants believed in

the divinity of Christ but only as part of a theological system or as a Person of the Trinity. His point was that Jesus Christ as Son of God and Messiah did not receive the pre-eminent place in the creeds of Protestantism.

35. Ibid., pp. 103-111.

36. Scott, "Address," pp. 32-33; and Scott, *He Nekrosis*, pp. 95-97.

37. Samuel Simon Schmucker, *Fraternal Appeal to the American Churches, with a Plan for Catholic Union on Apostolic Principles*, Edited and with an Introduction by Frederick K. Wentz (Philadelphia: Fortress Press, 1965).

38. Alexander Campbell, although not discussing the specific proposals made by Schmucker, approved of his endeavors. Campbell felt that Schmucker's plan was having an effect on church union by encouraging an open exchange of ideas and fostering a Christian spirit that was necessary for union to take place. See Alexander Campbell, "Union of Christians," *The Millennial Harbinger*, n.s. 3 (May 1839): 212.

39. See Anne Ayres, *The Life and Work of William Augustus Muhlenberg* (New York, 1880), pp. 263-267; and J.T. Addison, *The Episcopal Church in the United States, 1789-1931* (New York: Scribner, 1951), p. 178. The "Muhlenberg Memorial," which was presented to the House of Bishops in 1853, was his most significant contribution to the preservation of unity within his own denomination. Muhlenberg urged the low and high parties in the church to exist in harmony in one united church where a large measure of freedom was allowed in doctrine and liturgy. The Protestant Episcopal Church could be, in Muhlenberg's view, the basis for bringing about Christian unity with the other denominations in America.

40. The Evangelical Alliance was formed in London in 1846, and in 1867 a branch was established in America. It was a voluntary association of individuals working together in cooperative effort based on the spiritual union assumed to be existing among Christians. The Alliance was conservative theologically and had a nine-point creedal statement to which all participants gave assent. Alexander Campbell wrote a series of five articles in *The Millennial Harbinger* in 1847 concerning it. Although Campbell had some reservations about the Alliance, its creed, and basis for one's membership, he spoke favorably of it. He felt that the Alliance was a positive step towards the realization of Christian union in America and wanted to cooperate with them and other such associations as much as possible. See Paul A. Crow, Jr., "The Anatomy of a Nineteenth-Century United Church," *Lexington Theological Quarterly* 18 (October 1983): 3-15, for a succinct overview of these endeavors for church union in the nineteenth century.

41. Scott, *To Themelion*, pp. 3-5. See also p. 69, where Scott related the Creed to the unity that prevailed in the Early Church: "God . . . has wisely fixed our belief on the most stupendous truth — 'God manifest in the flesh'. When this was the sole creed of the Church, as in the primitive ages, she was one. If the Church departs from this principle of union she must shoulder the consequences, which are logically and inevitably division and strife. She can read this in the past; history is God teaching by example."

42. Ibid., pp. 33, 42, 106-107.

43. Scott's understanding of Christian union differed markedly from that of Schmucker at this point. Whereas Schmucker put forth twelve articles of faith as the basis of union, for Scott the messiahship of Jesus Christ was the sole Creed of Christianity.

44. Ibid., p. 113.

45. Scott, "Address," p. 31.

46. Scott, *To Themelion*, pp. 46-47.

47. Ibid., p. 42.

48. Ibid., p. 112.

49. Ibid., p. 47.

50. Ibid., pp. 125-126. Scott's understanding of the Ancient Gospel, the plan of salvation, and his concern for Christian union were significant for the Disciples of Christ in the nineteenth century. The strength of his theology lay in its rootage in the New Testament and the centrality of the Person of Jesus Christ. The preaching of these themes by Scott and subsequent Disciples ministers resulted in a phenomenal growth of the New Reformation in the nineteenth century.

51. Scott, "On the Millennium—No. 1," *The Christian Baptist* 3 (July 1826): 236-237.

52. See "Report of Walter Scott, the Evangelist of the Association," in Hayden, *Early History of the Disciples in the Western Reserve*, pp. 171-173. Scott began his address with these words: "Beloved Brethren — The Christian of the nineteenth century has been permitted to witness the accomplishment of wonderful events. Providence has stationed him on a sublime eminence, from which he can behold the fulfillment of illustrious prophecies, and look backward upon nearly the whole train of events leading to the 'Millennium,' " (Ibid., p. 171).

53. See H. Richard Niebuhr, *The Kingdom of God in America* (New York: Harper, 1937) for a study of the idea of the Kingdom of God and millennialism as it developed in America from the colonial days through the nineteenth century.

54. Hayden, *Early History of the Disciples in the Western Reserve*, p. 183.

55. See Whitney R. Cross, *The Burned-over District: The Social and Intellectual History of Enthusiastic Religion in Western New York, 1800-1850* (Ithaca, New York: Cornell University Press, 1950), pp. 287-321, for a treatment of Miller and his movement.

56. David Edwin Harrell, Jr., *Quest for a Christian America: The Disciples of Christ and American Society to 1866*, 1 (Nashville: The Disciples of Christ Historical Society, 1966): 39-48, has presented a summary of premillennial and postmillennial thinking among the Disciples leaders prior to the Civil War. Harrell has shown that Walter Scott, Barton W. Stone, and others adopted the premillennial view for a period of time, whereas Alexander Campbell maintained a consistent postmillennial position throughout the ante-bellum era. After the decline of the Millerites in the mid-1840's, the leaders of the Disciples followed Campbell and advocated postmillennialism.

57. See Scott, "The Second Coming of Christ: The Cloud," *The Evangelist* 3 (June 1834): 134-137, and (July 1834): 146-150.

58. Baxter, *Life of Elder Walter Scott*, pp. 393-396.

59. Harrell, *Quest for a Christian America*, 1:42-46. See also W. Barnett Blakemore, Jr., "Jesus is the Christ: Walter Scott's Theology," *The Christian Evangelist* 84 (October 1946): 1058.

60. Scott, *The Messiahship*, pp. 296-335.

61. See Edwin Scott Gaustad, *A Religious History of America* (New York: Harper, 1966), pp. 154-178, for an historical sketch of the idea of Manifest Destiny in America in the nineteenth century.

62. Scott, *The Messiahship*, pp. 296-332.

63. Ibid., pp. 114, 118.

64. Ibid., p. 119. Scott referred to certain passages in Daniel, which prophesied that governments would continue to exist in the millennium. He interpreted Dan. 2:34, "a stone cut out of the mountain without hands," as referring to the outer, political government. "The Son of Man coming in the clouds of heaven" in Dan. 7:13 symbolized for Scott the inner or religious government in the Kingdom of God.

65. Ibid., pp. 307, 313.

66. Ibid., pp. 321-322.

67. Ibid., pp. 334-335.

68. Ibid., pp. 297-298.

69. Baxter, *Life of Elder Walter Scott*, pp. 432-433.

70. Ibid., pp. 353-357. Baxter has preserved portions of Scott's tract. It was a response to Soame Jenyns, an English statesman, who had written an essay in which he attempted to show that patriotism was inconsistent with Christianity. Jenyns argued that patriotism was not a Christian virtue according to the teachings of Christ and the apostles.

71. Ibid., p. 353.

72. In support of this view of patriotism, Scott referred to Matt. 15:24; 16:19; Luke 19:41; 24:47.

73. Ibid., p. 356.

74. Ibid., p. 357.

75. See Jerald C. Brauer, *Protestantism in America: A Narrative History* (Philadelphia: Westminster, 1965), pp. 168-184, for a concise analysis of the political, social, and religious implications of the slavery issue during the ante-bellum period. See also Smith, Handy, and Loetscher, *American Christianity*, II:170-172, 191-195, for further discussion of the slavery and colonization questions.

76. Baxter, *Life of Elder Walter Scott*, p. 359. See also Harrell, *Quest for a Christian America*, I:128-129, for a discussion of the slavery issue among some of the prominent Disciples leaders in the ante-bellum period.

77. The correspondence and editorial exchange between Scott and Field in 1834-1835 has been thoroughly researched by Stevenson, *Walter Scott: Voice of the Golden Oracle*, pp. 149-156.

78. *The Evangelist* 3 (September 1834): 233.

79. Baxter, *Life of Elder Walter Scott*, pp. 434-440, has preserved a few introductory paragraphs of Scott's essay.

80. Ibid., pp. 434-435.

81. Ibid., pp. 435-438.

82. Ibid., p. 437.

83. Ibid., pp. 438-439.

84. Ibid., pp. 439-440.

85. Ibid., pp. 440-445.

86. Ibid., pp. 443-444.

CHAPTER SIX

WALTER SCOTT'S LEGACY: THE TREASURE AND THE VESSEL

But we have this treasure in earthen vessels, to show that the transcendent power belongs to God and not to us (II Cor. 4:7).

No death in my horizon, out of my own family, came more unexpectedly or more ungratefully to my ears than this of our much beloved and highly appreciated brother Walter Scott; and none awoke more tender sympathies and regrets. Next to my father, he was my most cordial and indefatigable fellow laborer in the origin and progress of the present reformation. We often took counsel together in our efforts to plead and advocate the paramount claims of original and apostolic Christianity. His whole heart was in the work. He was indeed, truly eloquent in the whole import of that word in pleading the claims of the Author and Founder of the Christian faith and hope; and in disabusing the inquiring mind of all its prejudices, misapprehensions and errors. He was, abusing the inquiring mind of all its prejudices, misapprehensions and errors. He was, too, most successful in winning souls to the allegiance of the Divine Author and founder of the Christian Institution, and in putting to silence the cavilings and objections of the modern Pharisees and Sadducees of Sectarianism.

He, indeed, possessed, upon the whole view of his character, a happy temperament. It is true, though not a verb, he had his moods and tenses, as men of genius generally have. He was both logical and rhetorical in his conceptions and utterances. He could and he did simultaneously address and interest the understanding, the conscience, and the heart of his hearers; and in his happiest seasons constrain their attention and their acquiescence.

He, without partiality or enmity in his heart to any human being, manfully and magnanimously proclaimed the truth, the whole truth, and nothing but the truth, as far as he understood it, regardless of human applause or of human condemnation. He had a strong faith in the person and mission, and work of the Lord Jesus Christ. He had a rich hope of the life everlasting, and of the inheritance incorruptible, undefiled and unfading.

I knew him well. I knew him long. I loved him much. We might not, indeed, agree in every opinion nor in every point of expediency. But we never loved each other less, because we did not acquiesce in every opinion, and in every measure. By the eye of faith and the eye of hope, methinks I see him in Abraham's bosom.

Alexander Campbell, The Millennial Harbinger,
1861, pp. 296 ff.

These words of Alexander Campbell express in a succinct way his tribute to and admiration for the man with whom he labored for forty years in the nineteenth century Reformation. Walter Scott left his mark on the movement of which he was a pioneer spirit.

In this study the attempt has been made to discuss Walter Scott's life, activities, thought, and contributions to the Independent Christian Churches, Churches of Christ, and Christian Church (Disciples of Christ). Here, we have focused on the biblical, theological, and philosophical currents that shaped his thinking, and in light of this heritage we have discussed the themes that were central in his understanding of the Christian faith.

A little over a century and a quarter has passed since the death of Scott. We now live in the latter decades of the twentieth century. Our view of the world has altered markedly since his day. As one looks back on Scott and especially the way he understood and formulated the Christian faith, one may be tempted to conclude that he has nothing of significance to say to the modern person. He is light years away from us in terms of the way he thought and expressed himself.

On second look, one would probably want to alter this judgment on Scott. As we stir through the embers of a fire that once was, we may still glimpse a few flickering sparks. For the day in which he lived, Scott was in many ways ahead of his time. What he had to say, the grand vision he had, and the major thrusts in his thinking may have vital relevance to our age and especially to those who stand in the Restoration tradition. Further, it is true that each generation must map out a course for the future. In this quest one searches out one's historical roots, in this case Walter Scott. Historical roots, then, are those inspirational sources or persons to whom one turns time and time again so as to grow new branches and limbs. Patrick Henry expressed this same truth when he said: "I have no light to illuminate the pathway of the future save that which falls over my shoulders from the past." Hopefully, this is true in the case of Walter Scott as the church looks to the future.

One may with justification be critical of certain features of Scott's thought. Some may consider his theology vulnerable at points, and he may have his detractors. However, the focus of this concluding evaluation will be in a different direction. Instead of searching out the inadequacies and limitations of his theology, the concern here will be positive and appreciative in a twofold way. First, the endeavor shall be to see where he made his major contributions to the nineteenth century Reformation in the formative years. Second, our focus will be on those aspects of his thought that are abiding and have theological significance for the church in the present era.

Walter Scott: The Mirror of a Movement

In his life and thought Walter Scott reflected the central concerns of the Reformation of the nineteenth century. One could well look upon him as the mirror of a movement and of the times in which he lived. But at the same time he left his mark on the movement as a pivotal figure.

All of the early leaders, Thomas and Alexander Campbell, Walter Scott, and Barton W. Stone, were educated men. They were preachers, teachers, writers, editors, and educators. It is significant that the New Reformation was spearheaded by men of such caliber, thoughtful and educated men, who exercised reasoned judgment in their understanding of the Christian faith. This concern for rationality has indelibly stamped the Restoration Movement as one with a reasoned approach to understanding the Scriptures and the central elements of the Christian gospel.

Walter Scott's writings were read by preachers in his own generation and in succeeding ones. His theology was influential in helping shape the style and content of preaching for future generations of Restoration ministers. This is especially true of his method of evangelism and the five-finger exercise.

From early days to the latter years of his life, Scott was a recognized and respected leader among the Disciples. He was an associate of the more prominent leader, Alexander Campbell, who held him in great respect. Scott was much sought after as a preacher and evangelist by the congregations of the movement and he was in a remarkable way able to communicate both with preachers and laypersons.

One may not agree with every detail of Scott's theology. However, there is much with which one must agree, founded as it is on Holy Scripture. In him one encounters a creative, fruitful mind, whose life and thought have profoundly shaped a religious movement. One cannot understand or appreciate the early history of the nineteenth century Reformation without seeing the important role Walter Scott played.

The Scriptures: Oracles of the Holy Spirit

Central to understanding the thinking of Walter Scott

is the important role of the Scriptures. For Scott and his associates in the New Reformation, Christian theology was formulated by reflecting on the Scriptures. In his attempt to interpret the meaning of the faith to persons in his own day, Scott sought his answers in conversation with the Scriptures, and he used them in his preaching and theological writings. Scott was scholarly in his approach to the Scriptures, and in his interpretation used the best biblical scholars of the day with whom he was acquainted. He appealed to that which was reasonable and substantiated by scriptural evidences, thereby presenting a rational, intelligible understanding of the Christian gospel. He set his understanding of the faith over against the emotionalism, subjectivism, and passivity in the current Calvinistic scheme of conversion.

Closely related to Scott's understanding of the Scriptures was his polemic against creeds. Jesus Christ as Messiah and Son of God was for Scott the Creed of Christianity, the central truth and only creed in the Scriptures. He set this affirmation over against the creedal statements and doctrinal formulations that were put forth by the Presbyterians (Westminster Confession of Faith) and Baptists (Philadelphia Confession of Faith). According to Scott and Campbell, it was not necessary to subscribe to the articles of these or other creeds in order to become a member of the church. The Scriptures enjoin a person only to have faith, repent, and be baptized to be a Christian and a member of the church. Scott advocated also that Christian unity could not be attained by subscribing to creedal statements or by adhering to prescribed theological formulations not based on the Scriptures.

Scott and his associates were correct in their view that creeds can be divisive when wrongly used. Schisms can develop when creeds become too rigid and are made the tests of fellowship in a church or the criterion for one's orthodoxy. The strength of the anticreedal sentiments of Scott and Campbell was that it guarded the freedom of the individual. It also emphasized that a relationship with the Person of Jesus Christ as witnessed to in Scripture, not giving assent to creedal propositions, is fundamental to the gospel.

Scott, the Campbells, and Stone have stamped the Restoration movement as one that has continued to find in Scripture the source of all the doctrines of the faith. Since the beginning of the movement the Scriptures have been basic, although the church has not always interpreted the faith in the manner of these early leaders. The Reformers came into being as a rationally oriented and biblically centered people, and have remained true to this heritage to the present day. As in Scott's day so in our age, the church is strongest and most vital when its message is grounded in a reasoned, faithful interpretation of the Scriptures. Christian theology will always be a dialogue with the Scriptures in light of the complexities of the political, social, and religious issues of the day. A reasoned, scholarly approach to the Scriptures and its message is needed in view of the irrationalism and overemphasis on emotion in much of our contemporary religious life. Also, this approach to Scripture is essential because of the alternatives posed by nonbiblical religions and various kinds of religious cults in our day.

Jesus Christ: Faith's Foundation

Walter Scott contributed to the Reformation of the nineteenth century in his emphasis on the centrality of Jesus Christ in the Scriptures, and this is one of the most significant aspects of his legacy. According to his reading of the New Testament, the Christian faith rests upon the fundamental truth that Jesus Christ is the Messiah and Son of God; this was the Golden Oracle and Creed of Christianity. In his thinking the coming of Jesus Christ was a fulfillment of the hopes and prophecies of Israel's faith. Hence, he found a significant place for the Old Testament in understanding the Christian faith. He did not, therefore, disregard the Old Testament or relegate it to a position of secondary importance as has been done by certain persons and movements in the history of the church.

The strength of Scott's position was that the Christian gospel focused on a person, the Christ of the New Testament, and one's belief in Him. His understanding of the Person of Jesus Christ contained rational elements (a truth to be proved by prophecies fulfilled and miracles performed) and personal ones (the individual's personal faith and commitment to Christ). Since Scott centered Christianity in a person and not a creed or theological system, this saved his theology from becoming a thoroughgoing rationalism. Hence, his theology was biblical and person centered.

Scott was correct in his attempt to show how in a fundamental sense the messiahship of Jesus Christ was the basis for understanding the other truths of the faith. The church was founded on the belief that Jesus Christ is the Messiah and Son of God (Matt. 16:16). The New Testament plan of salvation, or the Ancient Gospel, entailed faith in Jesus Christ as Messiah, and stemming from this were the six steps in the process of salvation (Acts 2:38). Christian union could be atttained if all the churches accepted as the basis of the gospel the fundamental truth of the messiahship of Jesus Christ and the other tenets of faith he taught (Eph. 4:4-6). In Scott's thinking it was the proclaiming of these biblical truths of Jesus Christ as the Messiah, the church, salvation, and Christian union that gave to preaching its integrity and power.

For contemporary theological endeavor one must begin with the biblical truth that Jesus of Nazareth is the Messiah, the person who fulfills Israel's religious faith and hope. This was the insight of Walter Scott, and this truth has stamped the Movement with a certain distinctiveness. All of their beliefs are derived from Scripture and from the understanding of Jesus Christ as Messiah and Son of God. Membership in the Christian Church does not necessitate subscribing to a series of articles in a creed. One is simply to affirm one's belief that Jesus is the Christ, repent, and be obedient unto him through baptism. All of Christian theology in the final analysis is explicating, amplifying, and applying to one's own era the multiple meanings and implications of this basic belief concerning Jesus as the Christ. This is true of our understanding of revelation, the church, salvation, Christian union, and the other cardinal tenets of the faith.

Preaching the Ancient Gospel: The Heart of the Matter

Walter Scott's evangelistic preaching, especially on

the Western Reserve during the years 1827-1830, was particularly notable and contributed to the newly emerging movement for reform. His evangelistic efforts strengthened the churches in the Mahoning Baptist Association numerically during this period of time. Through Scott's preaching, the ideas of Alexander Campbell and the Reformers got into the churches at the grassroots level.

Scott's evangelism was unique in that it consisted in a rational and scriptural plan of salvation and a personal relationship to Jesus Christ as Messiah and Son of God. His efforts in preaching what he took to be the Ancient Gospel represented an alternative to the emotionalism, subjectivism, and passivity implied in the orthodox Calvinistic scheme of conversion. To persons of the Calvinistic persuasion who were experiencing doubts and uncertainties regarding the state of their souls, Scott preached in a straightforward manner that one does not have to remain passive or rely on feeling states. One may take steps toward one's salvation by reading the Scriptures, believing, repenting, and being baptized. By following this biblical plan, one may have positive assurances of salvation. Hence, in Scott's evangelistic preaching there was a sense of liberation from the creedalism, emotionalism, passivity, and the arbitrariness of God's eternal decrees of election and reprobation in the Calvinistic plan of salvation.

Scott was successful in his evangelistic preaching and was a pivotal figure in the separation of the Reformers from their Baptist moorings. Due in great part to Scott's preaching and personal influence, they were able to crystallize as a definite religious group within the

Mahoning Baptist Association. With the dissolution of the Association in 1830, they became an autonomous, identifiable group and were thus free to unite with the Christians under Barton W. Stone in 1832 and form a new religious movement.

In Scott's preaching there was the sense of having discovered for the church of his day a truth he thought had been lost for centuries. This awareness of discovery, coupled with the idea of the nearness of the end, gave to Scott a sense that his work along with the other Reformers was the dawning of a new era in the history of Christianity. They were on the threshold of something new — a plan of salvation and a plan that would unite the various denominations of his day through the restoration of Primitive Christianity. Scott and the Reformers looked upon themselves as part of a great drama in the history of the church, and in this drama they had a decisive role to play. These ideas gave to Scott's preaching a sense of urgency, expectation, and excitement. This enthusiasm was shared by those associated with him in the New Reformation and accounted in great part for the large number of converts he was able to make.

Scott's preaching of the Ancient Gospel, with the five-finger exercise in the plan of salvation, gave to the Reform movement an effective instrument for doing evangelism. His style and content set a pattern of preaching that was significant in the evangelistic activities of the Disciples. It was appropriated by the majority of preachers in the Movement during the early years and used with signal success. Scott gave to the Disciples the consciousness that evangelism is at the heart of the

Christian gospel and stamped the Movement as one in which a strong evangelistic appeal is central. One of the keys to the phenomenal growth of the Christians was the evangelistic method formulated by Scott. By 1850, over one hundred fifty thousand persons were members of reform minded congregations. Scott's method of evangelism was used throughout the nineteenth and into the twentieth century with a large measure of success.

As in Scott's day, so in the contemporary church, the Christian gospel has a rootage in that which is reasonable and intelligible, and there are steps one can take in response to the preaching of Jesus Christ. We can use Matt. 16:16 and Acts 2:38 in our evangelistic preaching, as Scott did in his own time, and see these passages as one of the most meaningful ways to preach the gospel. When these passages are used in preaching and are clearly and intelligibly interpreted, persons can be led to a trusting commitment of faith in Jesus Christ and a meaningful relationship with God.

Christian Union: A Vision of Oneness

For Walter Scott, as well as the Campbells and Stone, the question of Christian union was a principal concern. For them this was a necessity in light of the fragmentation and sectarian character of the churches of their day. It was their view that one needed to begin at the beginning; thus, they opted for a restoration of the church in the New Testament in order to achieve union. In Scott's thinking the basis of Christian union was the belief that

Jesus Christ is the Messiah and Son of God; he also expressed this in terms of the Lordship of Christ and "God manifest in the flesh." A belief in the Person of Jesus Christ was the "polar star of Christian union." Our unity has been given in Him and Christians must claim it (Eph. 4:4-6). All creeds and confessional statements were in his judgment divisive and could not be the basis of Christian unity as some individuals in his day were advocating.

In Scott's understanding of restoration, the churches would be constituted along the same lines, central to which was the plan of salvation or the Ancient Gospel. If all Protestants adopted his understanding of the church, sectarianism would be overcome, and Christian union would be realized. As Scott envisioned the united church, it was not a merger or an organic union. It entailed a relationship of mutual acceptance among the churches and their members. Christians could pass from one congregation to another and have a common, interchangeable membership. Churches were to cooperate with each other in various endeavors, and a spirit of love and peace was to prevail among the members. A belief in Jesus Christ as Messiah and Lord would bind all of the members together in unity. Hence, the kind of unity Scott called for was centered in the local congregations and their members. In order to bring about the kind of unity he envisioned, Scott called upon the Protestant churches to engage in a dialogue with one another in a convocation for unity. The basis for this convocation among the Protestant groups was their common commitment of faith in the Person of Jesus Christ as Messiah and Lord.

Walter Scott had a deep concern for effecting unity among the churches of his day and dedicated his energies to this end. Scott, the Campbells, and Stone were not able to accomplish Christian union in their time. They have, nevertheless, bequeathed to the Christian churches the continuing passion for and commitment to the union of all Christians. In this quest, they have set a direction that is at the heart of the thinking of the churches. In all of this questing, the church must be guided by the fundamental insight of Walter Scott and the other early leaders that the Person and Lordship of Jesus Christ as revealed in the word is the basis of all unity conversations and efforts. This is true for all Christian bodies today if conversations are to be meaningful and fruitful. Our unity is rooted in an understanding of the Person of Jesus Christ and seen in relationship to the New Testament. Further, Scott's insight has continuing validity in that unity must concern the local congregations and relationships of love and acceptance that should exist between all Christian people. Jesus Christ as Lord, and His word as guide, together compose the vital center of all genuine Christian unity, and by sharing in His life and spirit we are all made one, despite any diversities in non-essentials.

Conclusion

This study of Walter Scott and his theology has a valuable lesson to offer about the meaning of history and historical research. One of the principal tasks of theology is learning from the past and expressing in a new way the meaning of biblical faith in the light of contemporary concerns. As one probes the roots of one's religious heritage, in this case Walter Scott and the early Restoration Movement, one does see value. It is true that we cannot understand the present or plot a course for the future of the church without a backward glance to see where we have been. In many ways the problems Scott faced are not the same problems the church faces today; in other respects they are quite similar. The important thing is that one can see the way he approached his problems, what resources he brought to bear upon them, what insights he had, and how he expressed these truths.

Walter Scott was not a theologian who can be compared with the great minds of the church. In his theological understandings, he does not adequately measure up to the stature of Alexander Campbell or Barton W. Stone. However, as a theologian and as an evangelist, Scott made his mark on the Restoration Movement. Without seeing the contribution he has made or the valuable legacy he has left, one cannot adequately understand the movement historically. By claiming this legacy the church can receive valuable guidance in our day and see more clearly our future direction as the people of God. For these reasons Walter Scott rightly deserves an honored place as one of the Four Founding Fathers of the Christian Church.

SELECTED BIBLIOGRAPHY

I. Primary Sources

Books, Addresses and Other Works

Scott, Walter. "Address given before the American Christian Missionary Society, Cincinnati: American Christian Publication Society, 1854." *Report of Proceedings of the Convention of Churches of Christ, at the Anniversaries of the American Christian Bible, Missionary, and Publications Societies, Held in Cincinnati, October 17th, 18th, 19th, and 20th, 1854. Prepared for Publication by the Secretaries*, pp. 26-42.

_____. *The Autobiography of Walter Scott 1796-1861*. Edited and with a Foreword by Roscoe M. Pierson. Bosworth Memorial Library, The College of the Bible, Lexington, Ky., 1952. Reprinted by permission of the Editor by Carthage Christian Church, Cincinnati, Ohio, August, 1970.

_____. *Christian Psalms and Hymns*. With an addition by Silas W. Leonard, Teacher of Vocal Music, with Names of Appropriate Tunes. Jeffersonville, Ia., A.S. Tilden, 1839.

_____. *A Discourse on the Holy Spirit*. Second Edition, enlarged and improved. Bethany, Va., Alexander Campbell, 1831.

_____. *The Gospel Restored. A Discourse of the True Gospel of Jesus Christ, in which the Facts, Principles, Duties, and Privileges of Christianity are Arranged, Defined, and Discussed, and the Gospel in its Various Parts Shown to be*

Adapted to the Nature and Necessities of Man in His Present Condition. Cincinnati: Ormsby H. Donogh, 1836.

_____. *The Messiahship, or Great Demonstration, Written for the Union of Christians, on Christian Principles, as Plead for in the Current Reformation.* Cincinnati: H.S. Bosworth, 1859.

_____. "Moses and Christ. Redemption — A Type." *Pioneer Sermons and Addresses.* pp. 163-182. Compiled by F.L. Rowe, Assisted by M.A.C. Restoration Reprint Library. Cincinnati, Ohio: F.L. Rowe, 1908.

_____. *He Nekrosis, or the Death of Christ. Written for the Recovery of the Church from Sects.* Cincinnati: C.A. Morgan & Co., 1853.

_____. Personal Notebook, 1836-1847. Lexington Theological Seminary, Lexington, Kentucky.

_____. *Psalms, Hymns, and Spiritual Songs, Original and Selected.* Compiled by A. Campbell, W. Scott, B.W. Stone, and J.T. Johnson, Elders of the Christian Church. With Numerous and Various Additions and Emendations. Adapted to Personal, Family, and Church Worship, by Alexander Campbell, Second Edition. Bethany, Va.: A. Campbell, 1861.

_____. *To Themelion: The Union of Christians, on Christian Principles.* Cincinnati: C.A. Morgan & Co., 1852.

_____. "United States' System. An Address." *The College of the Bible Quarterly* 23 (April 1946): 4-44.

Articles by Walter Scott in Contemporary Restoration Periodicals*

Scott, Walter. "The Lord's Day." *The Apostolic Advocate* 5 (1834): 320.

_____. "A Discourse on Eternal Life." *The Apostolic Advocate* 5 (1834): 332-335.

_____. "On Teaching Christianity — No. 1." *The Christian Baptist*, 1955 ed. 1 (September 1, 1823): 30-32.

_____. "The Resurrection of Jesus Christ from the Dead." *The Christian Baptist*, 1955 ed. 1 (October 6, 1823): 59-62.

_____. "On Teaching Christianity — No. 2." *The Christian Baptist*, 1955 ed. 1 (November 3, 1823): 66-71.

_____. "On Teaching Christianity — No. 3." *The Christian Baptist*, 1955 ed. 1 (January 5, 1824): 110-114.

_____. "On Teaching Christianity — No. 4." *The Christian Baptist*, 1955 ed. 1 (February 2, 1824): 133-137.

_____. "Primitive and Modern Christianity." *The Christian Baptist*, 1955 ed. 2 (September 6, 1924): 23-29.

_____. "On the Millennium — No. I." *The Christian Baptist*, 1955 ed. 3 (July 3, 1826): 236-238.

_____. "On the Millennium — No. II." *The Christian Baptist*, 1955 ed. 4 (September 7, 1826): 25-26.

_____. "Experimental Religion." *The Christian Baptist*, 1955 ed. 4 (February 5, 1827): 141-143.

_____. "On Experimental Religion — No. II." *The Christian Baptist*, 1955 ed. 4 (June 4, 1827): 223-226.

_____. "Election — No. I." *The Christian Baptist*, 1955 ed. 6 (March 2, 1829): 177-179.

_____. "Election — No. II." *The Christian Baptist*, 1955 ed. 6 (May 5, 1829): 240-243.

_____. "Election — No. III." *The Christian Baptist*, 1955 ed. 7 (October 5, 1829): 69-73.

_____. "Election — No. IV." *The Christian Baptist*, 1955 ed. 7 (October 5, 1829): 73-77.

_____. "Formation of Christian Character." (Reprint

from *The Evangelist*). *The Christian Messenger*, ed. B.W. Stone and John T. Johnson. 6 (June, 1832): 185-188.

_____. "The Circus." (Reprint from *The Protestant Unionist*). *The Christian Record*, ed. James M. Mathes. 5 (July, 1847): 12-13.

_____. "Elements of Justification." (Reprint from *The Protestant Unionist*). *The Christian Record*, ed. James M. Mathes. 5 (July, 1847): 16-17.

_____. "New York German Catholic Seceders." (Reprint from *The Protestant Unionist*). *The Christian Record*, ed. James M. Mathes. 5 (July, 1847): 30-31.

_____. "The Downfall of Jerusalem." (Reprint from *The Protestant Unionist*). *The Christian Record*, ed. James M. Mathes. 5 (September, 1847): 68-69.

_____. "Extract of a Circular Letter." *The Millennial Harbinger* 1 (January 4, 1830): 34-35.

_____. "True Holiness." *The Millennial Harbinger* 1 (July 5, 1830): 325-328.

_____. "On Public Speakers." *The Millennial Harbinger* 1 (September 6, 1830): 419-421.

_____. "Marriage — No. I." *The Millennial Harbinger* 2 (March 7, 1831): 139-142.

_____. "Marriage — No. II." *The Millennial Harbinger* 2 (May 4, 1831): 202-206.

_____. "Cooperation of Churches — No. II." *The Millennial Harbinger* 2 (June 6, 1831): 241-242.

_____. "Cooperation of Churches — No. III." *The Millennial Harbinger* 2 (June 6, 1831): 243-246.

_____. "Do Thyself No Harm." *The Millennial Harbinger* 3 (January 2, 1832): 237-239.

_____. "The Body of Christ." *The Millennial Harbinger* 5 (January, 1834): 5-7.

_____. "Remarks on General Meetings." (Reprint from *The Evangelist*). *The Millennial Harbinger* 5 (September, 1834): 461-463.

_____. "Events of 1823 and 1827." (Reprint from *The Evangelist*). *The Millennial Harbinger* n.s. 2 (October, 1838): 465-466.

_____. "Extracts from the Evangelist." (Letters from Alexander Campbell and Walter Scott). *The Millennial Harbinger* n.s. 4 (April, 1840): 187-188.

_____. "The Evangelist." *The Millennial Harbinger* n.s. 4 (September, 1840): 415-419.

*The articles written by Scott in each of the five listed periodicals are listed according to their date of publication.

Periodical Literature Edited or Co-edited by Walter Scott

The Evangelist. Vol. 1, No. 1 (1832) through Vol. 2, No. 10 (1833). Cincinnati, Ohio.

The Evangelist. Vol. 2, No. 11 (1833) through Vol. 4, No. 7 (1835). Carthage, Ohio.

The Evangelist. Vol. 4, No. 8 through No. 12 (1835). Cincinnati, Ohio.

The Evangelist. Vol. 5 (1836). *The Gospel Restored*. Cincinnati, Ohio.

The Christian: A monthly publication, devoted to the Union of Protestants upon the Foundation of the Original Gospel and the Apostolic Order of the Primitive Church. Vol. 1, Co-edited with John T. Johnson. Georgetown, Ky., Stuart & Stark, Main-st., 1837.

The Evangelist. Vol. 6, No. 1 (1838) through Vol. 7, No. 10

(1839). Carthage, Ohio.

The Evangelist. n.s. Vol. 7, No. 11 (1839) through Vol. 8, (1840). Cincinnati, Ohio.

The Evangelist. n.s. Vol. 9 (1841) through Vol. 10 (1842). Carthage, Ohio.

The Carthage Evangelist. n.s. Vol. II, April 1843 through March 1844. Carthage, Ohio.

The Protestant Unionist. Co-edited with Robert H. Forrester. Vol. 1, No. 1 (1844) through Vol. 4, No. 31 (1848). (Robert H. Forrester last appears as Co-editor Vol. 3, No. 30, July 1847). Pittsburg, Pa.

The Protestant Unionist. Co-edited with T.J. Melish. Vol. 4, No. 32 through No. 52 (1848). (T.J. Melish becomes co-editor, Vol. 4, No. 38, September 9, 1848). Cincinnati, Ohio.

The Christian Age and Protestant Unionist. Co-edited with Robert H. Forrester. Vol. 5 (1849) through Vol. 6 (1850). Cincinnati, Ohio.

Personal Letters

Walter Scott. To Mrs. Dorothea Bryant (daughter of Thomas Campbell), Mayslick, Ky., May 8, 1860. *Memoirs of Elder Thomas Campbell, together with a Brief Memoir of Mrs. Jane Campbell,* Alexander Campbell. Cincinnati, H.S. Bosworth, 1861.

_____. To Brother Emmons, May's Lick, October 22, 1851. Letter of Elder Walter Scott, No. 120. From the files of Francis Whitefield Emmons. Nashville, Disciples of Christ Historical Society.

_____. To Philip S. Fall. Written during the years 1841-42. Nashville, Disciples of Christ Historical Society.

_____. To Elder I.T. Payne, Versailles, Ky. n.d. Nashville, Disciples of Christ Historical Society.

II. Secondary Sources

General Works

Abbott, B.A. *The Disciples: An Interpretation.* St. Louis: Christian Board of Publication, 1924.

Adamson, William R. *Bushnell Rediscovered.* Philadelphia: United Church Press.

Addison, J.T. *The Episcopal Church in the United States, 1789-1931.* New York: Scribner, 1951.

Ahlstrom, Sydney E. *A Religious History of the American People.* New Haven: Yale University Press, 1972.

An Alexander Campbell Reader. Introduced and Prepared by Lester G. McAllister. St. Louis: CBP Press, 1988.

Ayres, Anne. *The Life and Work of William Augustus Muhlenberg.* New York, 1880.

Bacon, Francis. *The New Organon and Related Writings.* Edited, with an Introduction, by Fulton H. Anderson. New York: Bobbs-Merrill Company, Inc., 1960.

Baird, Robert. *Religion in America.* A Critical Abridgement with Introduction by Henry Warner Bowden. New York: Harper, 1970.

Baird, William, *What Is Our Authority?* St. Louis: Christian Board of Publication, n.d.

Baptism, Eucharist, and Ministry. Faith and Order Paper No. III. Geneva: World Council of Churches, 1982.

Baxter, William. *Life of Elder Walter Scott.* The Walter Scott Centennial Edition. Abridged by B.A. Abbott.

St. Louis: Bethany Press, 1926.

_____. *Life of Elder Walter Scott: With Sketches of His Fellow-Laborers, William Hayden, Adamson Bentley, John Henry, and Others.* Cincinnati: Bosworth, Chase, & Hall, 1874.

Beecher, Lyman. *Views in Theology.* Published by Request of the Synod of Cincinnati, 2nd ed. Cincinnati: Truman and Smith, 1836.

Benson, George. *A Paraphrase and Notes on the Epistles of St. Paul to Philemon, 1st Thessalonians, IId Thessalonians, 1st Timothy, Titus, IId Timothy. Attempted in Imitation of Mr. Locke's Manner.* London: Printed for Richard Ford, at the Angel in the Poultry, over-against the Compter, 1734.

_____. *A Paraphrase and Notes on the Seven (commonly called) Catholic Epistles. Viz. St. James, I St. Peter, II St. Peter, St. Jude, I, II, and III of St. John. Attempted in Imitation of Mr. Locke's Manner. To Which are annexed Several Critical Dissertations.* London: Printed and Sold by J. Waugh, in Gracechurch-street, 1749.

Blakemore, William Barnett. *The Discovery of the Church: A History of Disciple Ecclesiology.* Nashville: Reed and Company, 1966.

Boles, H. Leo. *Biographical Sketches of Gospel Preachers.* Nashville: Gospel Advocate Company, 1932.

Boston, Thomas. *Human Nature in Its Fourfold State, of Primitive Integrity, Entire Depravation, Begun Recovery. And Consummate Happiness or Misery. Subsisting in the Parents of Mankind in Paradise, the Unregenerate, the Regenerate. All Mankind in the Future State. In Several Practical Discourses.* Edinburgh: Printed for the Booksellers, 1794.

Brauer, Jerald C. *Protestantism in America: A Narrative History.* Philadelphia: Westminster Press, 1965.

Brougham, Henry Lord. *A Discourse of Natural Theology, Showing the Nature of the Evidence and the Advantages of the Study.* Philadelphia: Carey, Lea, and Blanchard, 1835.

Brown, John T. *Churches of Christ.* Louisville: John P. Morton and Company, 1904.

Bushnell, Horace. *Building Eras in Religion.* New York: Scribner, 1881.

_____. *God in Christ: Three Discourses Delivered at New Haven, Cambridge, and Andover, with a Preliminary Dissertation on Language.* New York: Scribner, 1910.

_____. *The Vicarious Sacrifice, Grounded in Principles Interpreted by Human Analogies,* 2 vols. New York: Scribner, 1891.

_____. *Work and Play.* New York: Scribner, 1883.

Campbell, Alexander, ed. *The Christian Baptist,* 7 vols. Buffaloe, Brook County, Va.: Printed and published by Alexander Campbell, 1827-1829. Nashville: Gospel Advocate Company, 1955.

_____. *The Christian Baptist.* Revised by D.S. Burnet, from the 2nd. ed., with Mr. Campbell's last corrections. 7 vols. in 1. Published by D.S. Burnet. Cincinnati: James and Gazlay, 1835.

_____. *The Christian System: In Reference to the Union of Christians, And a Restoration of Primitive Christianity, As Plead in the Current Reformation.* Nashville: Gospel Advocate Company, 1964.

_____. *A Debate on Christian Baptism, Between Mr. John Walker, a Minister of the Secession, and Alexander Campbell, to which is Added a Large Appendix.* Second Edition Enlarged. Pittsburg: Eichbaum and Johnson, 1822.

_____. *A Debate on Christian Baptism, Between the Rev. W.L. Maccalla and Alexander Campbell, in which are Interpreted and to which are added Animadversions on Different Treatises on the Same Subject Written by Dr. J. Mason, Dr. S. Ralston, Rev. A. Pond, Rev. J.P. Campbell, Rector Armstrong, and the Rev. J. Walker.* Buffaloe, Va.: Campbell and Sala, 1824.

_____. *The Millennial Harbinger.* 35 vols. Bethany, Va.: Printed and Published by the editor, 1830-1864.

_____. *The Sacred Writings of the Apostles and Evangelists of Jesus Christ, Commonly Styled the New Testament, translated from the Original Greek by George Campbell, James Macknight, and Philip Doddridge, with prefaces, various emendations, and an appendix by Alexander Campbell.* 3rd. ed. Bethany, Brooke Co., Va.: Alexander Campbell, 1832.

Campbell, George. *The Four Gospels, Translated from the Greek. With Preliminary Dissertations, and Notes Critical and Explanatory.* In 4 vols., With the Author's Last Corrections. Boston: W. Wells, and Thomas B. Wait and Co., 1811.

Campbell, Thomas. *Declaration and Address.* With an introduction by William Robinson. Birmingham, England: Berean Press, 1951.

Carson, Alexander. *Baptism in its Mode and Subjects Considered; and the Arguments of Mr. Ewing and Dr. Wardlaw Refuted.* New York: C.C.P. Crosby, 1832.

_____. *Miscellaneous Treatises.* New York: Hanna & Carson, At Theo. H. Gray's Printing Office, 1853.

_____. *The Works of Alexander Carson.* 4 vols. New York: Edward H. Fletcher, 1853.

Cassirer, Ernst. *The Philosophy of the Enlightenment.*

Translated by Fritz C.A. Koelln and James P. Pettegrove. Princeton: Princeton University Press, 1951.

Cheney, Mary Bushnell. *Life and Letters of Horace Bushnell*. New York: Harper, 1880.

The Christian Church (Disciples of Christ): An Interpretive Examination in the Cultural Context. Edited by George S. Beazley, Jr. St. Louis: The Bethany Press, 1973.

The Christian Portrait Gallery: Consisting of Historical and Biographical Sketches and Photographic Portraits of Christian Preachers and Others. Edited and published by M.C. Tiers. Cincinnati: Stereotyped at the Franklin Type Foundry, 1864.

Classic Themes of Disciples Theology. Edited with an introduction by Kenneth Lawrence. Fort Worth: Texas Christian University Press, 1986.

Cocceius, John. *Summa Doctrinae de Foedere et Testamento Dei*. Leyden: published in 1648.

Collingwood, R.G. *The Idea of History*. New York: Oxford University Press, 1957.

Copleston, Frederick. *A History of Philosophy*. Vol. 3: *Late Mediaeval and Renaissance Philosophy*. Pt. 2: *The Revival of Platonism to Suarez*. Garden City, New York: Image Books, 1963.

_____. *A History of Philosophy*. Vol. 5: *Modern Philosophy: The British Philosophers*. Pt. 1: *Hobbes to Paley*. Garden City, New York: Image Books, 1964.

Cross, Barbara M. *Horace Bushnell: Minister to a Changing America*. Chicago: University of Chicago Press, 1958.

Cross, Whitney R. *The Burned-over District: The Social and Intellectual History of Enthusiastic Religion in Western New York, 1800-1850*. Ithaca, New York: Cornell University Press, 1950.

Cummins, D. Duane. *A Handbook for Today's Disciples.* St. Louis: Bethany Press, 1981.

DeGroot, Alfred Thomas. *The Grounds of Divisions Among the Disciples of Christ.* A part of a dissertation submitted to the faculty of the Divinity School in candidacy for the degree of Doctor of Philosophy. Chicago: University of Chicago Libraries, 1939.

_____. *The Restoration Principle.* St. Louis: Bethany Press, 1960.

Dictionary of American Biography. Ed. Dumas Malone. Vol. 16. New York: Scribner, 1935.

The Dictionary of Bible and Religion. William H. Gentz, General Editor. Nashville: Abingdon, 1986.

A Dictionary of Christian Theology. Edited by Alan Richardson. Philadelphia: Westminster, 1969.

Dictionary of Christianity in America. Edited by Daniel G. Reid. Downers Grove, Illinois: InterVarsity Press, 1990.

Dictionary of National Biography. Edited by Leslie Stephen. Vol. 4. New York: Macmillan, 1885.

_____. Edited by Leslie Stephen. Vol. 8. New York: Macmillan, 1886.

_____. Edited by Leslie Stephen. Vol. 9. New York: Macmillan, 1887.

_____. Edited by Leslie Stephen. Vol. 21. New York: Macmillan, 1890.

_____. Edited by Leslie Stephen and Sidney Lee. Vol. 24. New York: Macmillan, 1890.

_____. Edited by Sidney Lee. Vol. 31. New York: Macmillan, 1892.

_____. Edited by Sidney Lee. Vol. 35. New York: Macmillan, 1893.

_____. Edited by Sidney Lee. Vol. 40. New York: Macmillan, 1894.

_____. Edited by Sidney Lee. Vol. 50. New York: Macmillan, 1897.

_____. Edited by Sidney Lee. Vol. 57. New York: Macmillan, 1899.

_____. Edited by Sidney Lee. Vol. 59. New York: Macmillan, 1899.

Dillenberger, John, and Welch, Claude. *Protestant Christianity Interpreted through Its Development.* New York: Scribner, 1954.

Disciples of Christ in the 21st Century. Edited by Michael Kinnamon. St. Louis: CBP Press, 1988.

Documents of the Christian Church. Selected and Edited by Henry Bettenson. London: Oxford University Press, 1971.

Doddridge, Philip. *The Rise and Progress of Religion in the Soul: Illustrated in a Course of Serious and Practical Addresses.* With an Introductory Essay, by John Foster. Boston: Perkins, Marvin, & Co., 1835.

Duke, James O. *What Sort of Church Are We?* St. Louis: Christian Board of Publication, n.d.

Encyclopaedia of Religion and Ethics. Edited by James Hastings. Vol. 3. New York: Scribner, 1951.

The English Philosophers from Bacon to Mill. Edited, with an Introduction, by Edwin A. Burtt. New York: Random House, 1939.

Errett, Isaac. *Linsey-Woolsey and Other Addresses.* Cincinnati: Standard Publishing Company, 1893.

Evangelism: Mandates for Action. Edited by James T. Laney. Hawthorn Books, Inc. New York: W. Clement Stone, 1975.

Finney, Charles G. *Lectures on Revivals of Religion.* ed. William G. McLoughlin. Cambridge, Mass.: 1960.

_____. *Memoirs of Rev. Charles G. Finney, Written by Himself.* New York: 1860.

Fisher, Edward. *The Marrow of Modern Divinity.* Edinburgh: John Gray and Gavin Alston, 1767.

Fortune, A.W. *Adventuring with Disciple Pioneers.* St. Louis: Bethany, 1942.

_____. *The Disciples in Kentucky.* Published by the Convention of the Christian Churches in Kentucky, 1932.

Frei, Hans W. *The Eclipse of Biblical Narrative: A Study in Eighteenth and Nineteenth Century Hermeneutics.* New Haven: Yale University Press, 1974.

Garrison, Winfred Ernest. *Alexander Campbell's Theology: Its Sources and Historical Setting.* St. Louis: Christian Publishing Company, 1900.

_____. *An American Religious Movement: A Brief History of the Disciples of Christ.* St. Louis: Bethany Press, 1945.

_____. *Christian Unity and Disciples of Christ.* St. Louis: Bethany Press, 1955.

_____. *Heritage and Destiny: An American Religious Movement Looks Ahead.* St. Louis: Bethany Press, 1961.

_____. *Religion Follows the Frontier: A History of the Disciples of Christ.* New York: Harper, 1931.

_____. *Whence and Whither the Disciples of Christ.* St. Louis: Christian Board of Publication, 1948.

_____, and DeGroot, Alfred T. *The Disciples of Christ: A History.* St. Louis: Bethany Press, 1964.

Gaustad, Edwin Scott. *Historical Atlas of Religion in America.* New York: Harper, 1962.

_____. *A Religious History of America.* New York: Harper, 1990.

Gilbert, George Holley. *Interpretation of the Bible: A Short History.* New York: Macmillan, 1908.

Glas, John. *The Works of Mr. John Glas.* 5 vols. 2nd. ed. Perth: R. Morrison and Son, Vol. 1-4, 1782, and Vol. 4, 1783.

Gonzalez, Justo L. *A History of Christian Thought.* Vol. 3. *From the Protestant Reformation to the Twentieth Century.* New York: Abingdon, 1975.

Grafton, Thomas W. *Men of Yesterday.* With an Introduction by Benjamin L. Smith. St. Louis: Christian Publishing Company, 1899.

Gresham, Perry Epler. *Campbell and the Colleges.* Nashville: Disciples of Christ Historical Society, 1973.

Hagger, Thomas. *Heralds of Christian Unity: Being Brief Biographical Sketches of Some Pioneers of the Restoration Movement.* Melbourne, Victoria, Australia: Austral Printing & Publishing Co. Ltd., 1938.

Haldane, James Alexander. *Memoirs of the Lives of Robert Haldane of Airthrey, and of His Brother, James Alexander Haldane.* New York: Carter and Brothers, 1857.

_____. *Observations on Forbearance.* Edinburgh: J. Ritchie, 1811.

_____. *A View of the Social Worship and Ordinances Observed by the First Christians, Drawn from the Sacred Scriptures Alone: Being an Attempt to Enforce Their Divine Obligation; And To Represent the Guilt and Evil Consequences of Neglecting Them.* Edinburgh: J. Ritchie, 1805.

Haley, J.J. *Makers and Molders of the Reformation Movement.* With an Introduction by J.H. Garrison. St. Louis: Christian Board of Publication, 1914.

Hall, Colby D. *The "New Light Christians:" Initiators of the*

Nineteenth-Century Reformation. Fort Worth, Texas: Stafford-Lowdon Co., 1959.

Hall, Ruth. *Condensed History of the Carthage Christian Church: Cincinnati, Ohio.* Prepared for use at its 125th Anniversary Celebration on November 3, 1957.

A Handbook of Christian Theology: Definition Essays on Concepts and Movements of Thought in Contemporary Protestantism. New York: New American Library.

Hanna, William Herbert. *Thomas Campbell: Seceder and Christian Union Advocate.* Joplin, MO: College Press Publishing Co., n.d.

Harrell, David Edwin, Jr. *Quest for a Christian America.* Vol. 1: *The Disciples of Christ and American Society to 1866.* Nashville: Disciples of Christ Historical Society, 1966.

Hayden, A.S. *Early History of the Disciples in the Western Reserve, Ohio; with Biographical Sketches of the Principal Agents in Their Religious Movement.* Cincinnati: Chase & Hall, 1875.

Hervey, James. *Theron and Aspasio: or, A Series of Dialogues and Letters, Upon the Most Important and Interesting Subjects.* In 2 vols. London: J.F. Dove, 1825.

Holifield, E. Brooks. *The Gentlemen Theologians: American Theology in Southern Culture 1795-1860.* Durham: Duke University Press, 1978.

Hudson, Winthrop S. *American Protestantism.* Chicago: University of Chicago Press, 1961.

_____. *Religion in America.* New York: Scribner, 1965.

Humbert, John O. *A House of Living Stones.* St. Louis: CBP Press, 1987.

Humble, Bill J. *Campbell and Controversy.* Joplin, MO: College Press Publishing Co., 1986.

Interpreting Disciples: Practical Theology in the Disciples of Christ. Ed. L. Dale Richesin and Larry D. Bouchard. Fort Worth: Texas Christian University Press, 1987.

Jennings, Walter Wilson. *Origin and Early History of the Disciples of Christ.* Cincinnati: Standard Publishing Company, 1919.

Kershner, Frederick D. *The Restoration Handbook.* Cincinnati: Standard Publishing Company, 1918.

Knatchbull, Sir Norton. *Annotations upon some difficult Texts in all the Books of the New Testament.* Cambridge: 1693.

Kummel, Werner Georg. *The New Testament: The History of the Investigation of Its Problems.* Trans. S. McLean Gilmour and Howard C. Kee. New York: Abingdon, 1970.

Latourette, Kenneth Scott. *A History of Christianity.* New York: Harper, 1953.

Lectures in Honor of the Alexander Campbell Bicentennial, 1788-1988. Introduction by James M. Seale. Nashville: Disciples of Christ Historical Society, 1988.

Livingstone, James C. *Modern Christian Thought: From the Enlightenment to Vatican II.* New York: Macmillan, 1971.

Locke, John. *An Essay Concerning Human Understanding.* Philadelphia: James Kay, Jun. and Brother, n.d.

_____. *A Paraphrase and Notes on the Epistles of St. Paul to the Galatians, First and Second Corinthians, Romans, and Ephesians. To which is prefixed an Essay for the Understanding of St. Paul's Epistles, By Consulting St. Paul Himself.* Cambridge: Brown, Shattuck, and Company, 1832.

_____. *The Reasonableness of Christianity, as Delivered in the Scriptures.* Boston: T.B. Wait and Company, 1811.

_____. *The Reasonableness of Christianity with a Discourse of Miracles and Part of a Third Letter Concerning Toleration.* Edited, Abridged, and Introduced by I.T. Ramsey. London: Adam & Charles Black, 1958.

McAllister, Lester G. *Thomas Campbell: Man of the Book.* St. Louis: Bethany Press, 1954.

_____, and Tucker, William E. *Journey in Faith: A History of the Christian Church (Disciples of Christ).* St. Louis: Bethany Press, 1975.

McGiffert, A.C. *Protestant Thought Before Kant.* New York: Harper, 1962.

Mackintosh, Hugh Ross. *Types of Modern Theology: Schleiermacher to Barth.* New York: Scribner, 1937.

Macknight, James. *A Harmony of the Four Gospels: In which the Natural Order of each is preserved. With a Paraphrase and Notes.* 2 vols. The Second Edition, corrected and greatly enlarged. London: Printed for William Strahan, Richard Baldwin, William Johnston, Thomas Longman, and Robert Horsfield, 1763.

_____. *A New Literal Translation from the Original Greek, of all the Apostolic Epistles. With a Commentary, and Notes, Philological, Critical, Explanatory, and Practical. To which is added, A History of the Life of the Apostle Paul.* 6 vols. 2nd. ed. To which is prefixed, An Account of the Life of the Author. London: Printed for Longman, Hurst, Rees, and Orme, 1806.

Marty, Martin E. *The Infidel: Free Thought and American Religion.* Cleveland: World Publishing Company, 1961.

_____. *Righteous Empire: The Protestant Experience in America.* New York: Dial Press, 1970.

Mead, Sidney E. *The Lively Experiment: The Shaping of Christianity in America*. New York: Harper, 1963.

Moore, Edward Caldwell. *An Outline of the History of Christian Thought Since Kant*. London: Duckworth, 1947.

Moore, William Thomas. *A Comprehensive History of the Disciples of Christ*. New York: Fleming H. Revell, 1909.

Moseley, J. Edward. *Disciples of Christ in Georgia*. St. Louis: Bethany Press, 1954.

Neth, John Watson. *Walter Scott Speaks — A Handbook of Doctrine*. Berne, Indiana: Economy Printing Concern, 1967.

Neve, J.L. *A History of Christian Thought*. Vol. 2: *History of Protestant Theology*. O.W. Heick, with contributions by Dr. J.L. Neve. Philadelphia: Muhlenberg, 1946.

Nevin, John W. *The Anxious Bench*. Chambersburg, Pa.: 1844.

Newcombe, William. *An English Harmony of the Four Evangelists, Generally Disposed after the Manner of the Greek of William Newcombe*. Philadelphia: Kimber and Conrad, 1809.

Newton, Sir Isaac. *Observations upon the Prophecies of Daniel, and the Apocalypse of St. John*. In 2 pts. London: J. Darby and T. Brown, 1733.

Nichols, James Hastings. *History of Christianity, 1650-1950: Secularization of the West*. New York: Ronald Press Company, 1956.

Niebuhr, H. Richard. *The Kingdom of God in America*. New York: Harper, 1937.

_____. *The Social Sources of Denominationalism*. New York: World Publishing Company, 1957.

Niebuhr, Reinhold. *The Nature and Destiny of Man: A*

Christian Interpretation. New York: Scribner, 1951.

Olmstead, Clifton E. *History of Religion in the United States*. Englewood Cliffs, N.J.: Prentice-Hall, Inc., 1960.

Osborn, Ronald E. *Experiment in Liberty: The Ideal of Freedom in the Experience of the Disciples of Christ*. The Forrest F. Reed Lectures for 1976. St. Louis: Bethany Press, 1978.

_____. *The Faith We Affirm: Basic Beliefs of Disciples of Christ*. St. Louis: Bethany Press, 1979.

Pope, Richard M. *The Church and Its Culture: A History of the Church in Changing Cultures*. St. Louis: Bethany Press, 1965.

The Reformation of the Nineteenth Century. Edited by J.A. Garrison. St. Louis: Christian Publishing Company, 1901.

Religious Issues in American History. Edited by Edwin Scott Gaustad. New York: Harper, 1968.

The Renewal of Church: The Panel of Scholars Reports. Edited by W.B. Blakemore. Vol. 1: *The Reformation of Tradition*. Edited by Ronald E. Osborn. Vol. 2: *The Reconstruction of Theology*. Edited by Ralph G. Wilburn. Vol. 3: *The Revival of the Churches*. Edited by W.B. Blakemore. St. Louis: Bethany Press, 1963.

Richardson, Robert. *Memoirs of Alexander Campbell, Embracing a View of the Origin, Progress and Principles of the Religious Reformation which He Advocated*. 2 vols. Nashville: Gospel Advocate Company, 1956.

Russell, Bertrand. *A History of Western Philosophy and Its Connection with Political and Social Circumstances from the Earliest Times to the Present Day*. New York: Simon and Schuster, 1945.

The Sage of Bethany: A Pioneer in Broadcloth. Compiled by Perry E. Gresham. St. Louis: Bethany Press, 1960.

Sandeman, Robert. *An Epistolary Correspondence between Samuel Pike and Robert Sandeman. To which is now annexed, Mr. Pike's Address to the Church, Then Assembling in St. Martin's Le Grand, Now in Paul's Alley, London. Intended as a Conclusion to the Correspondence. Together with Mr. Sandeman's Thoughts on Christianity.* Whitehaven: B.N. Dunn, 1798.

_____. *Letters on Theron and Aspasio. Addressed to the Author.* In 2 vols. The Second Edition. With a Preface, and an Appendix. Edinburgh: Sands, Donaldson, Murray, and Cochran, 1759.

Schaff, Philip. *The Principle of Protestantism.* Translated from the German by John W. Nevin, 1845. Bard Thompson and George H. Bricker, Editors. Vol. 1 of *Lancaster Series on the Mercersburg Theology.* Philadelphia: United Church Press, 1964.

Schmucker, Samuel Simon. *Fraternal Appeal to the American Churches, with a Plan for Catholic Union on Apostolic Principles.* Edited and with an Introduction by Frederick K. Wentz. Philadelphia: Fortress Press, 1965.

Schweitzer, Albert. *The Quest of the Historical Jesus. A Critical Study of its Progress from Reimarus to Wrede.* New York: Macmillan, 1960.

Shaw, Henry K. *Buckeye Disciples: A History of the Disciples of Christ in Ohio.* St. Louis: Christian Board of Publication, 1952.

Short, Howard Elmo. *Doctrine and Thought of the Disciples of Christ.* St. Louis: Christian Board of Publication, 1969.

Smith, H. Shelton, Handy, Robert T. and Loetscher, Lefferts A. *American Christianity: An Historical Interpretation with Representative Documents.* Vol. 1: 1607-1820. New York: Scribner, 1963.

_____. *American Christianity: An Historical Interpretation with Representative Documents.* Vol. 2: 1820-1960. New York: Scribner, 1963.

Stevenson, Dwight E. "The Bacon College Story: 1836-1865." *The College of the Bible Quarterly.* 29 (October 1962).

_____. *Disciple Preaching in the First Generation: An Ecological Study.* Nashville: Disciples of Christ Historical Society, 1969.

_____. *Lexington Theological Seminary: 1865-1965.* St. Louis: Bethany Press, 1954.

_____. "Walter Scott and Evangelism." *Voices from Cane Ridge.* Compiled and edited by Rhodes Thompson. St. Louis: Bethany Press, 1954.

_____. *Walter Scott: Voice of the Golden Oracle: A Biography.* St. Louis: Christian Board of Publication, 1946.

_____, and Goodnight, Cloy. *Home to Bethphage: A Biography of Robert Richardson.* St. Louis: Christian Board of Publication, 1949.

Stone, Barton Warren. *History of the Christian Church in the West.* Lexington: The College of the Bible, 1956.

Sweet, William Warren *Revivalism in America.* New York: Abingdon, 1944.

_____. *The Story of Religion in America.* New York: Harper, 1950.

Swinney, Oram Jackson. *Restoration Readings.* Copyright 1949 by Oram J. Swinney.

Teegarden, Kenneth L. *We Call Ourselves Disciples.* St. Louis: Bethany Press, 1975.

A Theological Word Book of the Bible. Edited by Alan Richardson. New York: Macmillan, 1971.

Thomas, Cecil K. *Alexander Campbell and His New Version.* St. Louis: Bethany Press, 1958.

Tillich, Paul. *A History of Christian Thought.* Edited by Carl E. Braaten. New York: Harper, 1968.

_____. *Perspectives on 19th and 20th Century Protestant Thought.* Edited and with an Introduction by Carl E. Braaten. New York: Harper, 1967.

Towers, Joseph Lomas. *Illustrations of Prophecy: In the Course of which are elucidated many predictions, which occur in Isaiah, or Daniel, in the Writings of the Evangelists, or the Book of Revelation; And which are thought to foretell, among other Great Events, a Revolution in France, favourable to the Interests of Mankind, the Overthrow of the Papal Power, and of Ecclesiastical Tyranny, the Downfall of Civil Despotism, and the subsequent Melioration of the State of the World: Together with a large collection of Extracts, Interspersed through the work, and taken from Numerous Commentators; and particularly from Joseph Mede, Vitringa, Dr. Thomas Goodwin, Dr. Henry More, Dr. John Owen, Dr. Cressener, Peter Jurien, Brenius, Bishop Chandler, Sir Isaac Newton, Mr. William Lowth, Fleming, Bengelius, Daubuz, Whitby, Lowman, Bishop Newton, and Bishop Hurd.* 2 vols. London: 1796.

Tristano, Richard M. *The Origins of the Restoration Movement: An Intellectual History.* Atlanta: Glenmary Research Center, 1988.

Tuveson, Ernest Lee. *Redeemer Nation: The Idea of America's Millennial Role.* Chicago: University of Chicago Press, 1968.

Walker, Williston. *A History of the Christian Church.*

Revised by Cyril C. Richardson, Wilhelm Pauck, Robert T. Handy. New York: Scribner, 1959.

Warburton, William. *The Works of the Right Reverend William Warburton*. 12 vols. London: Luke Hansard & Sons, 1811.

Wardlaw, Ralph. *Discourses on the Principal Points of the Socinian Controversy*. Andover: Mark Newman Flagg and Gould, 1815.

_____. *A Dissertation on the Scriptural Authority, Nature, and Uses, of Infant Baptism*. Boston: Pierce and Parker, 1832.

_____. *Lectures on the Book of Ecclesiastes*. 2 vols. in 1. Philadelphia: W.W. Woodward, 1822.

_____. *Unitarianism Incapable of Vindication: A Reply to the Rev. James Yate's Vindication of Unitarianism*. Andover: Mark Newman Flagg and Gould, 1817.

Weisberger, Bernard A. *They Gathered at the River: The Story of the Great Revivalists and Their Impact upon Religion in America*. Boston: Little, Brown and Company, 1958.

Welch, Claude. *Protestant Thought in the Nineteenth Century*. Vol. 1: 1799-1870. New Haven: Yale University Press, 1972.

West, Earl Irvin. *The Search for the Ancient Order: A History of the Restoration Movement, 1849-1906*. Vol. 1: 1849-1865. Nashville: Gospel Advocate Company, 1949.

West, William Garrett. *Barton Warren Stone: Early American Advocate of Christian Unity*. Nashville: Disciples of Christ Historical Society, 1954.

The Westminster Dictionary of Christian Theology. Ed. Alan Richardson and John Bowden. Philadelphia: Westminster, 1983.

Wilcox, Alanson. *A History of the Disciples of Christ in Ohio.* Cincinnati: Standard Publishing Company, 1918.

Williams, D. Newell. *Ministry Among Disciples: Past, Present, and Future.* St. Louis: Christian Board of Publication, 1985.

Williamson, Clark M. *Baptism: Embodiment of the Gospel.* St. Louis: Christian Board of Publication, 1987.

Windelband, Wilhelm. *A History of Philosophy* Vol. 2: *Renaissance, Enlightenment, and Modern.* New York: Harper, 1958.

Witsius, Herman. *The Oeconomy of the Covenants, between God and Man. Comprehending a Complete Body of Divinity.* To which is prefixed, The Life of the Author. A new translation from the original Latin. 3 vols. New York: George Forman, 1798.

Yancey, Mrs. Robert M. *Disciples of Christ at May's Lick, Kentucky.* 1941.

Articles and Addresses

Austin, Spencer P. "Walter Scott and Bacon College: The Question of His Presidency." *The Christian Evangelist* 84 (October 23, 1946): 1055-1056.

Baxter, William. "Alexander Campbell and Walter Scott, as Preachers." *The British Harbinger* (September 1, 1869): 289-294.

Blakemore, W.B., Jr. "Jesus Is the Christ: Walter Scott's Theology." *The Christian Evangelist* 84 (October 23, 1946): 1056-1059.

_____. "New Levels of Historical Concern Among the Disciples of Christ." *Church History* 25 (September 1956): 270-281.

Carpe, William D. "Baptismal Theology in the Disciples of Christ." *Lexington Theological Quarterly* 14 (October, 1979): 65-77.

Crow, Paul A. Jr., "The Anatomy of a Nineteenth-Century United Church." *Lexington Theological Quarterly* 18 (October 1983): 3-15.

Davis, M.M. "Walter Scott and His Lieutenants." *Christian Standard* 44 (March 13, 1909): 467-469.

Errett, Isaac. "Fifty-Nine Years of History." *Christian Standard* 21 (June 12, 1886): 185.

Fortune, Alonzo Willard. "Address Given at the Walter Scott Portrait Unveiling." *The College of the Bible Quarterly* 19 (October 19, 1942): 6-15.

Gardner, Frank W. "Walter Scott and Bacon College." *The Christian Evangelist* 75 (March 25, 1937): 383-385.

Garrison, Winfred E. "Walter Scott's Contribution: Effective Evangelism." *The Christian Evangelist* 84 (October 23, 1946): 1050-1052.

Gilpin, W. Clark. "Witness to the Deeds of God: Ministry in the Disciples Tradition." *Mid-Stream* XXVI, No. 3 (July 1987): 265-272.

Harden, W.L. "Centennial Addresses Delivered in 1909." Indianapolis: W.L. Hayden, 1909.

Harrison, Richard L. Jr., "Early Disciples Sacramental Theology: Catholic, Reformed, and Free." *Mid-Stream* XXIV, No. 3 (July 1985): 255-292.

_____. "Places of Authority in the Disciples of Christ: An Historical Perspective." *Mid-Stream* XXIV, No. 3 (July 1987): 317-323.

Jennison, William. "The University of Chicago and the Disciples of Christ: The Development of Biblical Criticism." *Discipliana* 38 (Fall 1978): 41-47.

Jones, Willis R. "Four Men — One Purpose." An address delivered Sunday morning, May 7, 1967, at the Central Christian Church, Shreveport, Louisiana.

Kershner, Frederick D. "The History of Evangelism." *The Indiana Christian* 21 (July, 1934): 2-4.

_____. "Stars. Chapter 5 — Message of Walter Scott." *Christian Standard* 75 (May 4, 1940): 427-429, 443.

_____. "Stars. Chapter 5 — Message of Walter Scott." *Christian Standard* 75 (May 11, 1940): 450-451, 468.

_____. "Stars. Chapter 5 — Message of Walter Scott." *Christian Standard* 75 (May 18, 1940): 475, 479.

_____. "Walter Scott: The Prophet of New Testament Evangelism." An Address for Pastors Use. Indianapolis: Butler College, n.d.

Key, Thomas C. "The Gospel on Their Fingers." *Christian Standard*, 92 (October 13, 1956): 9.

Lard, Moses E. "A Monument to Walter Scott." *Lard's Quarterly* 2 (January 1865): 133.

Liggett, Thomas J. "Why the Disciples Chose Unity." *Lexington Theological Quarterly* 15 (January 1980): 24-31.

Loos, Charles Louis. "Walter Scott." *The Christian-Evangelist* 54 (January 17, 1907): 81-82.

North, Ross Stafford. "Walter Scott: Practitioner of Restoration." *The Restoration Principle: Being the Abilene Christian College Annual Bible Lectures 1962.* Abilene, Texas: Abilene Christian College Students Exchange, 1962.

Pearson, Samuel C. Jr. "Acontius and Unity — Many Years Before the Campbells Came Along." *The Disciple* (December 3, 1978): 8-9.

Porter, Calvin L. "Thinking Our Way into the Future

with the Truth Behind Our Backs." *Mid-Stream* XXVI, No. 3 (July 1987): 306-316.

Shaw, Henry K. "Eloquence in Frontier Evangelism." *Front Rank* 55 (October 27, 1946): 1-2, 12.

_____. "Walter Scott, the Evangelist and the Mahoning Baptist Association." *The Christian Evangelist* 84 (October 23, 1946): 1052-1055.

Snoddy, E.E. "Barton W. Stone and Walter Scott, Ambassadors of the Everlasting Gospel." Wichita Falls, Texas, Texas State Convention, 1931. Published copy in possession of the Disciples of Christ Historical Society, Nashville, Tennessee.

Stauffer, C. Roy. "Revivalism versus Evangelism." *Discipliana* 41 (Fall 1981): 35-46.

Stevenson, Dwight E. "Scott: The Pioneer Evangelist Speaks to Our Own Time of Spiritual Longing." *The Disciple* (November 20, 1977): 11-12.

_____. "Walter Scott — Spokesman for the 'Ancient Gospel.'" *The Disciple* (November 6, 1977): 38-39.

_____, and Booth, Osborne. "The Disciples' First College." *The Christian Evangelist* 74 (October 8, 1936): 1302-1303.

Todd, Joseph C. "Grave of Parents of Elder Walter Scott." *Christian Standard* 73 (October 8, 1938): 983.

_____. "Moffatt — Birthplace of Walter Scott." *Christian Standard* 73 (January 15, 1938): 53-54.

Ware, Charles Crossfield. "Walter Scott — Pioneer Editor: That Angel of the Tempest." *The Christian Evangelist* 84 (October 23, 1946): 1059-1061.

Watkins, Keith. "The Disciples Heritage in Worship." *Mid-Stream* XXVI, No. 3 (July 1987): 290-298.

Welshimer, P.H. "Walter Scott." *Christian Standard* 71

(March14, 1936): 249-250.

Wilburn, Ralph G. "The Background for Disciple Theology in North America: From Colonial Covenant Theology to the Great Revivals." *Lexington Theological Quarterly* 14 (January 1979): 19-32.

Williams, D. Newel. "The History of Disciples Evangelism: 'If I or an Angel Should Preach Another Gospel ...' " *Mid-Stream* XXVI, No. 3 (July 1987): 339-350.

Williamson, Clark M. "Disciples Baptismal Theology." *Mid-Stream* XXV, No. 2 (April 1986(: 200-223.

Wrather, Eva Jean. "My Most Cordial and Indefatigable Fellow-Laborer." Alexander Campbell Looks at Walter Scott, 1821-1961. Part 1. *The Christian Evangelist* 84 (October 23, 1946): 1044-1048.

_____. "My Most Cordial and Indefatigable Fellow-Laborer." Alexander Campbell Looks at Walter Scott, 1821-1961. Part 2. *The Christian Evangelist* 84 (October 30, 1946): 1074-1077.

Theses and Dissertations

Fishback, Vernon Len. "Some Influences of the Idea of the Messiahship in Walter Scott's Program of Church Life as Reflected in His Writings." B.D. thesis, School of Religion, Butler University, 1949.

Neth, John W., Jr. "An Introduction to George Forrester." B.D. thesis, School of Religion, Butler University, 1951.

_____. "An Investigation and Analysis of the Doctrine of Walter A. Scott." M.A. thesis, School of Religion, Butler University, 1950.

North, Ross Stafford. "The Evangelism of Walter Scott."

M.A. thesis, Louisiana State University, 1950.

Phillips, George Richard. "Differences in the Theological and Philosophical Backgrounds of Alexander Campbell and Barton W. Stone and Resulting Differences of Thrust in Their Theological Formulations." Ph.D. dissertation, Vanderbilt University, 1968.

Small, Edward T. "The Contribution of Walter Scott to the Disciples of Christ." B.D. thesis, Vanderbilt University, 1930.

Smith, Mary Agnes Monroe. "A History of the Mahoning Baptist Association." M.A. thesis, West Virginia University, 1943.

Williams, David Newell. "The Theology of the Great Revival in the West as Seen Through the Life and Thought of Barton Warren Stone." Ph.D. dissertation, Vanderbilt University, 1979.

Wilson, Herbert John. "The Contributions of Walter Scott to the Nineteenth Century Reformation." M.A. thesis, Butler University, 1941.

Catalogues and Indexes

An Author Catalog of Disciples of Christ and Related Religious Groups. Compiled by Claude E. Spencer. Canton, Mo.: Disciples of Christ Historical Society, 1946.

The Christian-Evangelist Index: 1863-1958. Vol. 3. Nashville: Disciples of Christ Historical Society, 1962.

Christian Standard Index: 1866-1966. Vol. 5. Nashville: Disciples of Christ Historical Society, 1972.

Theses Concerning the Disciples of Christ and Related Religious Groups. Compiled by Claude E. Spencer.

Nashville: Disciples of Christ Historical Society, 1964.

Letters

Librarian of the University of Edinburgh. To Dwight E. Stevenson, April 24, 1946. Nashville: Disciples of Christ Historical Society.

Robertson, Marjorie, Assistant Librarian, University of Edinburgh. To William A. Gerrard III, October 12, 1979. Nashville: Disciples of Christ Historical Society.

_____. To William A. Gerrard III, December 21, 1979. Nashville: Disciples of Christ Historical Society.

Yancey, Mrs. R.M. To R.J. Bamber, May's Lick, Ky., March 16, 1933. Disciples of Christ Historical Society.

Miscellaneous Church Records, Programs, and Minutes

Journal of the Mahoning Baptist Association. Minutes of the Meetings 1820 to 1826; Constitution of the Association; and articles of faith of the ten original member churches as well as others which were added in later years. Hiram, Ohio: Hiram College Library, n.d.

Printed copy of the minutes of the Mahoning Baptist Association and of the corresponding and circular letters sent to similar associations and member churches, 1821-1827. Cleveland, Ohio: Western Reserve Historical Society, n.d.

Program. National Evangelistic Association of the Churches of Christ. Memphis, Tennessee. City Auditorium, November 9-11, 1926. Indianapolis, Indiana: Library of the United Christian Missionary Society.

Small, Walter. "May's Lick Church Record." (original longhand copy) Lexington: Lexington Theological Seminary, n.d.